MYSTERIES *of* BLACKBERRY VALLEY

Where There's Smoke
The Key Question
Seeds of Suspicion
A Likely Story
Out of the Depths
Run for the Roses
Crooks and Christmas Cookies
Smoke and Mirrors
No Love Lost
The Cookbook Clue
The Final Cut
A Brush with Danger
The Mandolin Mystery

Bear with each other and forgive one another
if any of you has a grievance against someone.
Forgive as the Lord forgave you.

—Colossians 3:13 (NIV)

MYSTERIES *of* BLACKBERRY VALLEY

The Mandolin Mystery

CATE NOLAN

Guideposts

Published by Guideposts
100 Reserve Road, Suite E200
Danbury, CT 06810
Guideposts.org

Cover and interior design by Müllerhaus
Cover illustration by Bob Kayganich at Illustration Online LLC.
Typeset by Aptara, Inc.

ISBN 978-1-965859-11-7 (hardcover)
ISBN 978-1-965859-12-4 (softcover)
ISBN 978-1-965859-13-1 (epub)

Printed and bound in the United States of America
10 9 8 7 6 5 4 3 2 1

The Mandolin Mystery

Chapter One

Hannah Prentiss looked up as her fiancé, Liam Berthold, entered Jump Start Coffee on a sunny Friday morning in June. He had just finished an overnight shift as the chief of the Blackberry Valley Fire Department. Fatigue weighed on his shoulders, but a smile lit his face the moment his gaze settled on her. He detoured to greet her with a kiss before heading to the counter to place his order.

When he returned to the table, coffee and blueberry muffin in hand, Liam settled into the chair across from her. "You are a sight for tired eyes. Sorry I'm late."

"Rough night?" Hannah studied the creases etched into his face. His hair was still damp from the shower he must have taken at the end of his shift.

Liam nodded. "We were out at the campgrounds for hours after someone got a little overenthusiastic with a bonfire. It got out of control pretty quickly. The camp manager was smart enough to call for help, so damage was minimal. We stuck around to make sure there was no risk of it reigniting."

Hannah appreciated how conscientious Liam and all the firefighters were about protecting Blackberry Valley from fire danger, but she hated the toll it sometimes took on him. "You're free for the rest of the day and have a long nap planned, I hope?"

Liam grinned, and she knew that even though he protested, he loved that she fussed over him. "Yes, ma'am. That's why this is decaf. Unless another emergency arises, I have a date with my pillow. Jealous?" he teased.

Hannah laughed. She loved how easily they joked with each other. It was one of the perks of being great friends as well as being in love.

She sobered. "I hope nothing for the festival was damaged."

Liam gave her a reassuring smile. "No, the campground is set far back from the stage they're building. It was never a threat."

"That's a relief. It would be a shame if the festival had to be canceled, especially because of something like that. I've heard people are coming from all over for it."

Blackberry Valley was set to host the revival of a traditional bluegrass festival in just over a week. The original festival had gone on every year for a decade, until it abruptly ended in the seventies because the founding duo split in an ugly feud. Now the grandson of the original promoter had booked a long weekend of performances to celebrate the fiftieth anniversary of the last show. Some veteran performers would be there, along with a number of up-and-coming acts. Anticipation ran high in town at the prospect of an influx of tourists and musical artists.

"Jacob has been digging into bluegrass culture, hoping to create some signature dishes. I think he and Marshall are cooking up something together," Hannah said as she sipped from her own cup, which was not decaf. She needed the energy for her busy day. Jacob Forrest—head chef at Hannah's restaurant, the Hot Spot—was known for his creativity, and local food critic Marshall Fredericks often spurred him on.

"I'm glad Marshall's back." Liam smothered a yawn.

"You and Raquel both. She's been humming bluegrass tunes as she serves our patrons." Hannah glanced at the clock on the wall. "Speaking of bluegrass, I need to head over to the library in about ten minutes. Evangeline Cooke asked us to be there by nine to begin setting up an exhibit."

"For the festival?"

"Yes. Eddie Conley's wife is friends with Evangeline and Phyllis Taft of the historical society. Mrs. Conley told them there was a shack full of memorabilia from the festival out at their farm. Phyllis originally planned a small display, but there were so many crates and containers that they decided to do a special commemorative display in the main library instead."

"Eddie was part of the original duo, right?"

Hannah laughed as she set down her mug. "Bonus points for the boyfriend. Eddie was the mandolin player."

"Fiancé," Liam corrected. "Soon-to-be husband." He reached across the table and took Hannah's hand in his. "I can't wait to marry you, but I love that we have mornings like this—just the two of us together with no talk of wedding plans."

Hannah basked in his gentle smile. "Thank you for suggesting the break. I'm keeping a list of the things we need to make decisions on—guests, venue, catering, flowers, and of course a dress." She stopped and took a breath. "It's a little overwhelming, but we have time. For now, I want to enjoy being together, cherishing everything I love about you."

"I love you too." The words slid off his lips so easily that it was hard to believe there had ever been a time she'd been unsure of his affection.

"Are you planning to come to the Hot Spot for dinner tonight?" Hannah asked.

"Missing me already?"

Hannah laughed. "Guilty as charged."

"Why don't I come with you to see if Evangeline and Phyllis need more help?"

"I thought you needed sleep," Hannah reminded him.

"After being out on the festival grounds last night and now hearing about the memorabilia shed, I'm intrigued. It reminds me of our visit to the Bluegrass Hall of Fame when we were searching for your great-uncle Chuck last fall. Besides, I'm feeling more energized now. Your smile gives me more of a kick start than Zane's coffee."

Hannah smiled as she shook her head. "No surprise when you're drinking decaf."

Liam waved away her protest. "Decaf has no effect on my love for your smile. So, should I come help?"

Hannah agreed, happy to have his company for a little longer. Once they'd finished their refreshments, they waved goodbye to Zane and headed over to the library. It was a short and pleasant journey as they strolled hand in hand, greeting friends they met along the way.

They were halfway up the library steps when a voice caught Hannah's attention. "Hannah Prentiss?"

Hannah looked around to see who called her name. When she saw a stylish young woman with wavy strawberry-blond hair dressed in a denim skirt and cowboy boots hurrying toward the steps, a broad smile broke across her face. "Monroe Taylor? Is that you? I haven't seen you since our first high school reunion. Well, except on television. I hear you're taking the country music world by storm."

Monroe ducked her head in the demure way Hannah remembered. It was funny to think of her performing in front of thousands of fans. She'd always been so shy in school.

"Are you here for the festival?" Hannah asked. "Please tell me you're performing."

"I am. I'll do some sets with my mom and then some of my own with my band."

Liam still stood by the door, so Hannah made introductions. "Liam, this is Monroe Taylor. We were friends all the way back in kindergarten. She's the granddaughter of Eddie Conley, who we were talking about earlier. Monroe, meet Liam Berthold, Blackberry Valley's fire chief and my fiancé."

"A pleasure to meet you, Monroe." Liam inclined his head as he greeted her. He'd been two years ahead of them in school, so he and Hannah had run in different circles.

"And you too, Liam. Congratulations!" she exclaimed as she embraced Hannah. Then she studied Liam. "I think I remember your father. Didn't he used to do visits to the elementary school? Stop, drop, and roll."

"That's right. I'm glad you remember what he taught you." Liam held the door open for them.

They stepped into the main room of the library, which currently bore no resemblance to the quiet sanctuary of books and readers Hannah had come to expect. Pandemonium reigned. Boxes were stacked against the wall and crates overflowing with instruments and posters formed a line down the middle of the room. Evangeline, looking somewhat flustered, ushered a few crying children and their harried mothers into the children's section. She collared one of the young volunteers to read a story. When she turned back toward the main room, Hannah caught a look of resignation on her face.

In the middle of the chaos stood the seventy-eight-year-old director of the historical center, Phyllis Taft, cool as a cucumber, directing volunteers as they unpacked the boxes.

Evangeline approached Hannah. "I'm so glad to see you. And Liam, you are a blessing. There are some bigger crates that need moving." She rolled her eyes at Monroe. "When your grandmother told me she had memorabilia, I never expected all this." Evangeline took a deep breath and slowly released it as Hannah patted her shoulder. "I'm trying to stay positive, and one thing is certain—we are going to give Blackberry Valley an exhibit to remember."

"What can we do to help?" Monroe asked.

"I'm deferring to Phyllis on this," Evangeline replied. "As director of the historical center, she's technically in charge. You might be able to help organize though. Do you know anything about what's in these crates?"

Monroe shook her head sadly. "As far as I know, it was all stored away fifty years ago and hasn't been touched since. I can't even imagine the condition some of it must be in."

"It won't be that bad," Evangeline assured her. "Your grandmother told me she had some storage company go through it in the early eighties. It was clear there would be no more festivals, but she didn't have the heart to get rid of everything. The workers put things into the proper protective cases." She glanced around. "It's a shame, but I just don't know where we're going to find places to display all of this."

"I have an idea," Hannah said. "With your grandparents' permission, Monroe, we could display some of the posters at the Hot Spot. My dad might even be able to make up another display case for some of the smaller, less valuable items."

"The Hot Spot?" Monroe gave her a questioning look.

"It's the farm-to-table restaurant I own here in town. Your grandmother sometimes joins Evangeline and other friends there for dinner."

"Hannah converted the old firehouse," Evangeline explained.

"Really? That sounds amazing."

"Amazing is exactly the word to describe the food her chef turns out," Liam said. "I highly recommend the—"

Hannah cut him off. "Don't trust any of his recommendations unless you have a high tolerance for spice. But you will have to come by and visit. Liam's right. My chef, Jacob Forrest, is a whiz in the kitchen, and he's working on some specials for the festival."

"Oh, that sounds tempting."

"Hey, Hannah." Lacy waved from across the room where she and her mother, Christine, were going through a box of news clippings.

"Lacy Johnston?"

"Monroe? How lovely to see you. And it's Lacy Minyard now." Lacy pushed away from the table and stood, smoothing her light maternity dress before she eased through the maze of boxes toward them. She hugged her girlhood friend as best she could with her belly between them. "It is so good to see you."

"And you. Look at you! When is the baby due?"

Lacy beamed. "Very soon. Well, actually, it just feels that way. I still have two months to go. You're in town for the festival, right? Are you performing?"

Monroe repeated the explanation she'd given Hannah.

"That sounds like so much fun," Lacy gushed. "What about your granddad? Is he going to make an appearance? You know the question on everyone's mind is whether we'll see a reunion of the Blackberry Mountain Boys."

Monroe's face fell, and she shook her head. "I'm sorry people will be disappointed, but he won't appear. He hasn't performed much since the last night of the festival in '76, the night his mandolin was stolen along with all the proceeds from the weekend. From what I've been told, it was as if the light went out of him. The band broke up that night, and Nana says he hasn't been the same since."

Hannah grimaced. "I can't even imagine. But don't worry about letting people down. We'll have lots of other great acts, including Monroe Taylor."

Monroe shot Hannah a grateful smile. "Okay, let's see what we can do to help Mrs. Taft make something special out of all of this."

"Oh, Monroe." Phyllis welcomed her with a one-armed hug as she juggled a clipboard and pen in her other hand. "You're just the person I've been waiting for. I need someone to help sort through this crate of instruments. I was thinking we could make an informational display showcasing the types of instruments traditionally played in a bluegrass band. Hannah, I was thinking of what you've done with the fire department memorabilia at the Hot Spot. I was going to use the photos here, but then this crate of instruments showed up, and that'll be so interesting visually." She gestured to the open crate sitting in a corner.

"We can do that, right, Monroe?"

"Sure. I lean more toward country, but I grew up surrounded by bluegrass, so I definitely know all the instruments." They headed for the corner and got right to work.

"What do you think about pulling everything out and spreading it on this study table so we can see what we've got?" Hannah suggested.

"Sounds good to me. What was Phyllis talking about that you did at your restaurant?"

Hannah reached into the crate to lift out a battered old banjo case. "About a year ago, shortly after I opened the Hot Spot, we got a rather savage review from the local restaurant critic. It was a good learning experience for us. One of the things he criticized was that 'the theming felt generic, like one might find in a chain restaurant anywhere in America.'" Hannah used her fingers to make air quotes. "And yes, I memorized every critical word so I knew what to fix. We all worked hard to do better, and now we're a success."

"So how did you update the theme?"

Hannah grinned. "Liam, his grandfather, and my dad took care of that. Liam's grandfather used to be fire chief. He sent Liam with a box of old photos and newspaper clippings and even his grandmother's diary. My dad made a display case. Marshall Fredericks—he's the food critic—was right in his critique. If you're going to convert the old firehouse into a restaurant and theme your menu accordingly, then the decor should reflect it. And now it does, as you'll see when you visit."

"Can't wait." Monroe lifted a case from the crate and handed it to Hannah, who opened it and set the guitar on the table. "I wonder why all these instruments are in here. I'll have to ask my grandparents. Maybe they were backups for the band members, but then why didn't those members keep them?"

"What's that?" Hannah asked when Monroe opened up the next case. It was some kind of guitar with a fancy metal front that looked like a hubcap.

"That's a Dobro. It's an acoustic guitar with a resonator that gives bluegrass its distinctive metallic sound. We use it in country music too."

"Is that everything?" Hannah asked as she set the Dobro on the table. There was no reply. When she glanced back, Monroe was staring intently at the instrument she was holding. "Is something wrong?"

Monroe sank onto a stool and cradled the instrument in her arms as she glanced up. Her voice shook as she spoke. "Hannah, this is Grandpa Eddie's missing mandolin."

Hannah gaped. "But how? I mean I thought it was stolen."

"It was. But I'm holding it in my hands right now."

"Are you sure?"

Monroe nodded slowly. "Without a doubt. I grew up surrounded by photos of Grandpa playing this mandolin. I used to study the images, trying to understand what was so special about it. See this little mark here?" She pointed to a slight indentation on the scroll. "Apparently, Grandpa Eddie had a tendency to rub it when he was getting ready to play. He wore it down with his thumb over the years. And this little scratch?" She laughed. "Nana said her kitten was trying to play with it and wasn't happy when Grandpa took it away."

Hannah chuckled at the mental image.

Monroe's fingers reverently stroked the maple neck, but she suddenly jerked them away as if she'd been burned. She lowered her head and closely examined the mandolin. Her voice sounded confused when she continued. "This was not the way it looked in the photos. This instrument has been broken and glued back together."

"What?"

"Look."

Hannah knelt beside her and examined the section Monroe pointed to. "That *is* glued, and they didn't even do a good job." She peered up at her friend. "What do we do now?"

Monroe blew out a breath. "I don't know. I want to take it to Grandpa Eddie, but I guess we should call the sheriff first. He'll know what to do."

Hannah nodded. "That's a good idea. Besides, I have some questions. Where did this mandolin come from? Who put it in this crate? Was it the person who stole it?" She paused as a thought occurred to her. "Didn't you say the mandolin and money were stolen together?"

Monroe's eyes grew wider as she followed Hannah's line of thinking. "If the mandolin and money were stolen together, where is the money?"

Chapter Two

For a long moment Hannah and Monroe stared at each other before Hannah broke their silence. "We'd better have Evangeline call Sheriff Steele."

Monroe gingerly set the mandolin on the table. "I hope I didn't destroy any fingerprints. How long do fingerprints last anyway?"

Hannah shrugged. "I have no idea, but don't feel bad. You couldn't have known. I imagine the storage company people left fingerprints too, plus anyone else who handled it fifty years ago."

"I don't think so." Monroe shook her head. "From what I've heard, no one was allowed to touch Grandpa Eddie's precious mandolin. According to family legend, the mandolin was given to Grandpa by Bill Monroe, the father of bluegrass himself. He and my great-grandfather were friends. When Bill heard young Eddie playing some banged-up banjo, he gave him his mandolin and told him to see what kind of music he could make with it. I guess he recognized Grandpa's talent. He promised they'd play together someday."

"Is that where your name came from?"

"Probably, though no one has actually said so." Monroe shifted her gaze back to the mandolin resting on the table. "I really wish I could take this straight to Grandpa Eddie. I want to see his face when he holds it in his hands again." She sighed in resignation.

"You're right though. Evangeline needs to call the sheriff, because this was stolen and the money is still missing."

"I completely agree," Hannah said.

Monroe glanced around the room. "I'll just stay here and watch over it if you'll go get her." She gave Hannah a sheepish look. "It's not that I think anyone here would actually take it, but now that it's found, I don't want to let it out of my sight before I can take it home to Grandpa."

Hannah understood Monroe feeling protective. "I'll be right back."

She left Monroe standing guard and went in search of the librarian, who seemed to have disappeared. After asking a few people if they had seen her, Hannah finally found Evangeline speaking with Liam by the back door. Liam had rolled up the sleeves of his white button-down shirt. There was just something about those strong arms that always got to Hannah. Every once in a while she would let herself imagine his arms holding their child one day, and—

"Hi, Hannah. Did you need something?" Evangeline asked.

Hannah yanked herself from her daydream. "Unfortunately, I need you to call the sheriff."

Liam was all business. "Can I help?"

Hannah shook her head. "This requires the sheriff, not the fire chief. You'll never believe this, but Monroe and I found the missing mandolin in the box of instruments we were sorting."

"The mandolin that was stolen fifty years ago?" Evangeline asked. "How do you know?"

"Monroe recognized it. But get this. It was broken and badly repaired. Monroe wanted to take it straight to her grandfather, but we figured it's evidence in an unsolved crime, so that means we need the sheriff."

"I can call if you want," Liam offered to Evangeline, who looked a little stunned.

"Yes, thank you, Liam." She turned to Hannah. "Where is the mandolin now?"

"Monroe is watching over it. She didn't want to risk anything happening to it."

"I'll say not. After all this time, who would ever believe? And in my library, no less." Evangeline gathered herself. "Let's go see this legendary mandolin."

Liam stepped outside to make the phone call while Hannah and Evangeline headed back into the main library, where they found that a crowd had gathered in the corner where Monroe sat with the instrument.

"Hannah! Can you believe it?" Lacy called when she saw them approaching. "Can you believe after all these years of thinking it was stolen, it was just here in this crate?"

Hannah wasn't sure it was that simple, but she was distracted from her thoughts when she realized the crowd was jostling for a chance to see the no-longer-missing mandolin. Someone needed to take control of the situation before an enthusiastic onlooker bumped into the table and knocked the instrument onto the floor.

"Liam is calling Sheriff Steele, but could everyone please back up a little until he gets here?" she asked. "We wouldn't want any harm to come to this before Eddie Conley gets to see it again."

Monroe shot Hannah a grateful glance as the volunteers backed away. "I shouldn't have said anything, but Lacy came over to chat. I told her, someone overheard, and I suppose everyone got excited."

"Of course they did," Hannah said. "It's an exciting find."

Liam approached them with the news that the sheriff was on his way. "He asked me to secure the scene until he gets here, but I see someone already took care of that." He winked at Hannah.

Sheriff Colin Steele arrived quickly, and Evangeline ushered him to the table where Monroe and Hannah waited. He greeted Hannah, who introduced him to Monroe. Then he sat down at the table across from her with the instrument between them.

"This is the mandolin?" At Monroe's nod, he continued. "How do you know it's the one that was stolen?"

Monroe repeated what she had told Hannah about the markings. "This mandolin reached a sort of mythic status in our family. I've seen more photos than you can count, and I've watched old family videos of my grandfather playing it. I have no doubt that this is his mandolin."

Colin nodded thoughtfully. "I know a little bit of the story because it's been a hot topic of conversation around town ever since the first rumors of a new festival surfaced. I'd like you to fill me in on the story as you know it."

Monroe hesitated. "That's a little hard. What I know doesn't come directly from my family, even though what happened obviously impacted them tremendously. Maybe that's why no one talked about it. My grandfather was crushed by what he considered the betrayal of his friends. He's a good man, but he knows how to hold a grudge. He held this one silently within himself. The Blackberry Mountain Boys were never mentioned in the house." She caught herself. "I'm sorry. I'm rambling because I don't know how to explain it. The mandolin disappeared, the money was stolen, and the band broke up. That's the simple version."

Colin made a few notations, then addressed Monroe again. "You said you know things that didn't come from your family. What is the source of that knowledge, and how reliable is it?"

Monroe gave a short laugh as she considered the question. "I'm in the music business myself. People have long memories, and they like to talk. Once this festival was announced, a lot of old rumors resurfaced. How reliable the stories are, I can't say, but there are some points that are reported fairly consistently. The first part is local history, so it's fact. In the late sixties, my father and his Blackberry Mountain Boys decided to jump on the bluegrass festival bandwagon and hold one right here in their hometown. The first festival was a modest success, but it sparked an interest, and over the next decade it grew into a popular annual event. In 1976, everyone was buzzing about the upcoming bicentennial, so the festival had a more Americana approach and was larger than ever. But that was the year everything went wrong." Monroe tilted her head. "Do you want me to keep talking, or would you rather hear the next part from my grandfather?"

Colin stroked his chin as he considered her question. "Give me what you've heard about what went down. That will prepare me to talk to your grandfather."

Hannah caught the sheriff's eye. She had a feeling that what he was really saying was that he wanted to hear the "industry talk," so he could compare it to whatever version he would hear from Eddie

Conley—and he wanted it before Monroe's version could be filtered by family loyalty.

Monroe bit down on her bottom lip as she appeared to consider how to begin. "As far as I know, everything was going well at the festival, but trouble was brewing behind the scenes. Back then, bluegrass musicians faced a tough choice. They could keep playing acoustic music and do small local tour circuits, or they could amplify their sound and be more successful in larger arenas. I don't know how familiar you are with music history."

"I know about as much as the ordinary person, but if this is important, give me an insider's understanding," the sheriff replied.

Monroe settled back in her seat, and Hannah noticed that she seemed more in her element explaining about music than she had rehashing family history.

"It was a turbulent time in music. Rock and roll had literally electrified things, allowing artists to be clearly heard in huge concert venues. A few bluegrass groups like the Osborne Brothers raised their popularity well beyond the traditional audience by changing over to amplified sound. Other bluegrass groups and fans saw that as a betrayal of their roots. It was a do-or-die time for a lot of artists. Record labels and radio stations didn't see any commercial value in traditional bluegrass, so some artists were mixing genres. The Blackberry Mountain Boys were caught up in the conflict. My grandpa was a purist, and he was against amplifying their sound. It wasn't really that he was against change. It was that music was his heart and soul. It was personal, and he believed that amplifiers destroyed the close connection he could establish with a small crowd." She gave a crooked smile. "Am I boring you yet?"

Colin shook his head. "Not at all. It's fascinating. Keep going. What caused the conflict?"

"I'll try to keep this short, because I really am anxious to take the mandolin to Grandpa. My grandfather, Eddie Conley, founded the Blackberry Mountain Boys along with Howard 'Ward' Burton. Other band members came and went over the years, but Grandpa and Ward were the face of the band. From what I heard, Ward was getting antsy. He was frustrated with Grandpa, because he wanted to amplify their sound and Grandpa wouldn't even discuss it. Ward had ambitions beyond local gigs. He was friends with some of the guys playing the big arenas, and he wanted that grandeur for himself. He and Grandpa were headed for a rift long before the mandolin disappeared. Rumor had it that this festival would be their last performance as a band."

"That wasn't all that surprising though, was it?" Hannah interjected. "When Liam and I visited the Bluegrass Hall of Fame last year, I learned that there were a lot of changeovers in bands."

"That's true," Monroe agreed. "Still happens today. Usually it's not a big deal, but Grandpa Eddie and Ward had been friends and partners since they were teenagers."

"So what turned this breakup into a feud?" Colin asked.

Monroe pointed to the mandolin. "When Grandpa's precious mandolin disappeared, he accused Ward of stealing it."

Chapter Three

Hannah felt a sudden shift in the atmosphere of the room and realized how many people had been listening.

Colin seemed to take note as well. He twisted in his chair to face Liam. "Will you call down to the station and ask them to send Jacky over? I'm going to need help taking statements from all these people."

Liam gave a single nod, then walked away to find a private location to make the call.

The sheriff turned back to Monroe and lowered his voice. "I don't want to make a scene by clearing the room. That will just get them talking. But let's save any sensitive information for when we are in private. As soon as Deputy Holt gets here, I'd like you to accompany me to your grandfather's house."

There was something about the way he said it that made Monroe's eyebrows rise, and even Hannah had a moment's hesitation. Was Colin suspicious of something Monroe had said, or was he just doing his job and covering all bases?

"Hannah?"

"Yes, Colin?"

"You were here with Ms. Taylor when she discovered the mandolin?"

The serious tone of the sheriff's voice struck Hannah. She was being questioned. She gathered her thoughts so she could answer carefully yet truthfully. "I was. Phyllis Taft asked us to use the instruments in this crate to create a display about the sounds of bluegrass. We were removing them and spreading them out on the table to see what we had to work with when Monroe discovered the mandolin in the crate."

"How far down would you say it was?"

Hannah gestured to the instruments on the table. "These two banjos, the fiddle, and the Dobro were on top of it. Once we found it, we didn't remove anything else."

Colin nodded and bent over to peer into the storage crate. "I see at least as many instruments still in there, so whoever placed it inside seems to have buried it so it wouldn't be seen."

"Maybe, maybe not," Hannah suggested.

Colin looked up from the crate. "What makes you say that?"

"Several reasons. These cases are not from fifty years ago. Evangeline told us that Eddie's wife hired a storage company in the eighties to preserve everything once it became clear there would be no more festivals. So it's entirely possible that whoever put the mandolin in there was merely an employee who had no idea he was handling a stolen instrument."

Colin scratched the back of his neck as he contemplated the information. "Most likely, whoever took the money spent it a long time ago, but we can't rule out the possibility that an employee of the storage company found it in the shed, then decided to take it and bury the mandolin in this box."

Hannah was intrigued by that idea. Colin was probably right that the money was long gone, but as she looked around the room, she realized there was still another possibility. "Unless the money is in one of these crates we haven't unpacked yet."

Her words brought a frown to the sheriff's brow and unleashed a fury of curious whispers among those close enough to hear.

Colin cast a look at the crowd, then leaned toward Hannah and spoke in a near whisper. "Do you have any reason for suspecting that?"

Hannah suddenly wished she'd kept her thoughts to herself. "Not really. As I was listening to your reasoning, I was thinking how random it was that Monroe—probably the only person in the room who would have recognized the mandolin—was the one who found it. I mean if Phyllis had asked someone else to set up the exhibit, it would have gone unnoticed for much longer. There are plenty of other boxes and crates here that haven't been opened yet, so who knows what else we will find? And on that note, I'll stop talking and leave you to investigate."

Colin let out a belly laugh that surprised Hannah. "You are going to stop and let me investigate on my own? Who are you and what have you done with Hannah Prentiss?"

She joined in the laughter at her own expense. "Fair enough. I'm not saying that I don't want to know more."

Colin grinned at her. "Never stop thinking and asking questions, Hannah. You've got a knack for figuring things out, and I value your thoughts." At Hannah's smile, he continued, "I just need you to be careful about crossing any lines. Deal?"

She stuck out her hand. "Deal."

Deputy Jacky Holt arrived and stole the sheriff's attention.

Hannah found Monroe staring at her in amazement. "Are you some sort of assistant to the sheriff?"

Hannah chuckled. "Nothing that official. I told you about my restaurant but didn't mention that I have another hobby of sorts. Since I've been back, I've somehow developed a talent for finding mysteries—or rather, they find me. I've been lucky and managed to solve a few."

"Don't let her humility distract you, Monroe," Liam said, coming up beside her. "Hannah is quite the detective. She's solved more than a few mysteries that left others in this town stumped. If anyone can figure out what's going on here, it's Hannah."

She smiled at Liam. "Spoken like the good fiancé you are."

He kissed her temple. "Nope, spoken like a man who admires your special talent, and considers himself lucky enough to be engaged to an amazing detective."

Hannah laughed. "Now that's laying it on a bit thick."

"If that's all I can be accused of, I'm a happy man. Oh, the sheriff needs me. Be right back."

As Liam walked away, Monroe's gaze followed him. When she turned back, Hannah noticed a sadness in her eyes. "Is something wrong?"

Monroe forced a smile. "Nothing other than my being nervous about Grandpa Eddie's reaction to the broken mandolin. You'll come with me to the house, won't you?"

Hannah made a face. "I don't think so. It will be difficult enough for your grandfather without having a stranger in the house."

"You're no stranger to him," Monroe protested. "Remember all the times we would spend out at his house, with my grandmother making sprinkle muffins for us?"

"Her muffins were the best," Hannah reminisced. "I always wondered how she got those colors inside. Isn't it funny how something so simple could seem magical to a kid?"

"Please say you'll come." Monroe clasped her hands together. "For old times' sake. I really need you." Her eyes twinkled as she added, "Besides, you'll need to hear Grandpa Eddie's version of the story if you're going to solve the mystery."

Chapter Four

Colin didn't seem at all surprised when Hannah accompanied Monroe to his cruiser, but he gave a little chuckle. "Just couldn't resist, could you?"

"I begged," Monroe piped up.

"I promise I'll just listen, if that's okay," Hannah added. "I'll admit that I'm pretty curious to see Mr. Conley's reaction to the news and hear what he has to say about it. I hope it makes him happy, even if the mandolin is broken."

The sheriff held the door for them, and Hannah and Monroe climbed into the rear seat of the police car. Monroe giggled softly as she carefully rested the mandolin's makeshift case on the seat between them. "I feel like we're back in high school being dragged home to our parents for some infraction."

"What did you get up to in high school?" Hannah teased. "I never had a sheriff bring me home."

"Me either, but I remember seeing it in a movie. I guess we're finding out what we missed out on."

Hannah looked at Monroe and burst into laughter. For a moment it did feel like they were back in school, just two girls having fun together. That illusion vanished the moment Colin put the key in the ignition and started the car.

"So, Ms. Taylor, why do you think your grandfather accused his friend of stealing a priceless instrument?"

Monroe appeared thoughtful. "I don't think he really meant it," she finally answered. "I think those were words said in the heat of the moment. But words hurt, and that accusation was the knife that made the final cut in their partnership."

Hannah hated to hear of any friendship ending.

Monroe apparently did too, as her shoulders dropped. "Music lost a talented duo, but the greater loss was their friendship. They'd grown up together, and music was the basis of their relationship. They'd learned to play at the feet of some of the greatest musicians in bluegrass, and the bond they shared was everything to them. I think it was the loss of Ward's friendship that drained Grandpa's joy, more than the loss of his mandolin or the money."

"Can you elaborate on that?" Colin asked.

Monroe shifted uneasily. "It's just my opinion. But, as I mentioned, from all reports, they were really struggling with the direction of the band. That night was the straw that broke the camel's back. I think it was easier for my grandfather to blame their breakup on the loss of the mandolin rather than on his own stubbornness."

"Did Eddie ever apologize for accusing Ward, since you say he didn't believe Ward had actually stolen it?"

"You'll have to ask him. I've never heard anything about that."

"Back to the talk in the industry for a moment," Colin continued. "Did anyone else float theories of who took the mandolin and the money, or why?"

"Do I have to answer that?"

Hannah caught Colin's gaze in the rearview mirror. She could see he was as surprised by Monroe's answer as she was.

"Is there a reason you don't want to?"

Monroe chewed on her lip again. "I don't want to cast aspersions on a person based on hearsay."

The sheriff nodded. "I promise to keep in mind that it's nothing more than industry gossip, but I'm faced with a decades-old crime that is suddenly new again. I'd appreciate any information, even if it's unfounded."

Monroe sighed. "Okay, but keep in mind that the rumor was probably fueled by Grandpa Eddie's accusation. Some people speculated that Ward took the money to front his new band."

"How long after the breakup did he form a new band?"

"Less than a month."

The cruiser was silent following the impact of that revelation. Hannah was the first to speak. "I know nothing about the music industry. Does it cost money to form a band?"

"Not if you're just a group of guys hanging out in a garage jamming, but if you want to get a record deal or go on tour, you need a promoter, a manager, studio fees, equipment, tour buses—the list goes on."

"Wouldn't Ward have had money from his success with the Blackberry Mountain Boys?" Hannah asked.

"Maybe, but according to the gossip, Ward had a reputation for living above his means. Supposedly, he loved fancy cars and had other expensive tastes. If you want to know if that's true, I guess you should ask Grandpa or talk to Ward. His son is performing in this festival as a way to honor the original performers, so he can tell you where to find Ward. I think he lives near Lexington now."

Hannah mulled over that information as the police cruiser wound through the streets of Blackberry Valley. "I realize I don't really know any of the players personally, and maybe I'm naïve, but it doesn't sit right with me that a man would do something like that to his close friend just because he wanted to start a new band."

Monroe shrugged. "As I said, it was only rumor. It doesn't feel right to me either. I don't know if he was ever officially a suspect, but you can probably find that out, right, Sheriff?"

"Yes, I'll go through the old case files. But it sounds like Ward moved on pretty quickly."

"Maybe, or maybe the split was already in the works. I've always assumed anger made it easier for Ward. Having his best friend publicly accuse him had to sting. He went on to huge success as the front man for a new band, but I wonder if he ever got over the loss of their friendship. His songs afterward all had a lonesome quality that became his signature."

Hannah's heart ached for the two men whose friendship had been severed. She couldn't imagine losing Lacy like that, and just today she'd learned that her friendship with Monroe had survived years of separation. Both of these men were in their eighties now, but wouldn't it be wonderful if somehow the discovery of the mandolin could heal the breach in their relationship? She knew it wouldn't be that easy, but she could hope and pray. And wonder—if Ward hadn't taken the money or broken the mandolin, who had?

Monroe's phone rang. She pulled it out and glanced down at the screen. "That's my grandmother. May I take it?"

"I'd rather you didn't," Colin replied. "We'll be there soon, and I'd prefer you not tip them off as to why we're coming."

Monroe let the call go to voicemail, then anxiously waited to read the transcript. "Too late. She already knows, and she's pretty upset that I didn't call her." She groaned. "Someone at the library must have called. Why didn't I realize that would happen?"

Hannah rested a reassuring hand on Monroe's arm. "You were busy being interviewed by the sheriff. Your grandmother will understand."

Colin was clearly frustrated that he hadn't thought of it either. He sped up, and shortly they were pulling up the long drive to the Conleys' home. Hannah recalled how she'd loved coming here as a child. The house was beautiful, set back behind a grove of trees, with a gorgeous view overlooking Blackberry Valley.

Thinking on it now, she realized it was amazing that the Conleys had lived in a house so easily accessible without the massive security that celebrities today needed to keep their families safe. It had been such a different time.

Mrs. Conley stood in the front doorway as they pulled into the circular drive. Monroe had barely gotten the car door open before the white-haired woman was making her way across the porch, leaning on her cane with one hand and clutching her skirt with the other to keep it from blowing in the summer breeze. "Monroe, what in the world is going on? Vera told me you found your grandfather's mandolin. Why didn't you call me? Why is the sheriff bringing you here? Are you in trouble?"

Monroe dashed up the path. "I'm not in any trouble. I'm so sorry. I would have called, but I've been with the sheriff." She hugged her grandmother. "Oh, Nana, can you believe it? I did find the mandolin. But it's not all good news." She looked around. "Is Grandpa here? Does he know?"

Mrs. Conley shook her head. "No, he's been out at the pond fishing, and I didn't want to say anything until I heard it from you."

Hannah stepped forward, cradling the mandolin case in her arms. She was glad Monroe was there to hold her grandmother steady, because the elderly woman looked on the verge of collapse when she realized what Hannah was carrying.

Tears glistened in her eyes as she asked, "Is that it?" At Hannah's nod, she turned back to Monroe. "Are you sure?"

"I am, Nana. It has the kitten's scratch."

"Oh my. After all this time." She leaned heavily against Monroe. "Where was it?"

"In one of the crates you sent to the library."

Colin came up the steps behind Hannah and removed his hat. "Ma'am, sorry to trouble you, but this is an active criminal case again, so I do need to speak to you and your husband. Your granddaughter has been good enough to give me some history, but I will need to interview you both separately."

Hannah thought Mrs. Conley paled at the sheriff's words, but that was understandable given how shocked she must be.

But Mrs. Conley lifted her chin. "Of course, Sheriff. Where are my manners? Please come in out of the sun. Monroe, why don't you go down and fetch your grandfather from the dock?"

Colin looked unsure of this plan. "Can I trust you not to tell him why I'm here, Ms. Taylor?"

Monroe nodded solemnly. "Hannah can come with me if you prefer."

The sheriff nodded his approval, so Hannah handed him the mandolin case and joined Monroe, heading around the back of the house. "What are you going to tell your grandfather?"

"I think I'll just tell him Nana needs him up at the house. He dotes on her, so he'll come even if he grumbles about his fishing being interrupted."

The two friends hurried across the back lawn that sloped down to a good-size pond. "I remember the winter you had a skating party on this pond during a deep freeze," Hannah observed. "I was secretly jealous that you had a skating rink in your backyard."

"And I was jealous that you lived closer to town. Funny the things that were so important to us back then. Hannah, I'm so glad you were the one with me when I found the mandolin. It makes it easier to have a friend nearby, you know?"

"I'm glad I was there too. I mean, finding a mandolin that's been missing for fifty years is pretty exciting on its own, but knowing it belonged to your grandfather and how important it was to him just makes it that much more special. And I have so many questions about what happened."

Monroe laughed. "I guess that's why you're so good at solving mysteries." She sobered as they crested a small hill. Her grandfather sat in his chair at the end of the dock he'd built especially for fishing. "He spends hours out here every day. I think he sings to the fish."

"Does he catch anything?"

"Nana keeps the pond stocked, but Grandpa throws back everything he catches." She grinned. "There are probably generations of fish living in that pond now. I guess he has a fish fan club."

Hannah's laughter made Eddie Conley turn around, and his face creased in a huge smile. "Monroe, how's my favorite grandchild?"

"I'm his only grandchild," Monroe whispered to Hannah. She called back, "I'm right as rain, Grandpa, but Nana needs you up at the house."

Mr. Conley grumbled as predicted, but he set his fishing pole aside, closed his tackle box and joined them. "Hello, Hannah Prentiss. It's been a long while since I saw you."

Hannah hadn't expected him to remember her. "Hi, Mr. Conley. I guess you need to join your wife for a visit to my restaurant. She says my chef does barbecue just the way you like it."

"Call me Eddie, Hannah. You're far too grown to be calling me Mr. Conley. I don't get out much, but Bev does know my likes, so maybe I will visit your restaurant. What brings you here today?"

Hannah exchanged a quick glance with her friend. "I was at the library setting up a display and ran into Monroe. We've been catching up."

He sighed. "For the festival? Don't know why anyone thought reviving that was a good idea."

Hannah wasn't sure how to reply to Eddie's comment, but she was saved from responding when he kept talking.

"Last one didn't end so well, but I guess people remember it fondly. And this year they'll get a chance to hear my girls sing." He chucked Monroe under the chin.

"Will you be in the audience for that?" Hannah held her breath, waiting for his answer.

"Not on your life. I can have a private concert anytime I want, right, Monroe?" Without waiting for an answer, he broke into the first line of "Wayfaring Stranger."

Monroe joined in on the second line, and they alternated back and forth as the trio made their way back toward the house.

When they finished, Hannah clapped her hands. "That was gorgeous. Thank you, Mr.—I mean, Eddie. I always loved hearing you sing that when I was young." In fact, listening to him sing around the house had been such a normal part of her visits that it wasn't until she'd grown older that she realized what a special treat it had been. To her, he'd just been Monroe's grandfather.

"Learned it at the knee of the great Bill Monroe himself. He always said—" Eddie broke off when he caught sight of the police cruiser. "Is Bev hurt? What's the sheriff doing here?"

"Nana's fine, Grandpa. The sheriff just came about something that happened in town."

There was more grumbling as Hannah and Monroe followed him up the stairs. "I knew no good would come of bringing that festival back to town."

Chapter Five

Eddie Conley was spry for his age, so Hannah and Monroe had to hustle up the stairs behind him.

"Beverly, where are you?" he called as he stepped through the door. "Are you okay?"

Monroe made a face and shrugged at Hannah. "He won't believe me until he sees her himself."

Mrs. Conley appeared in a doorway. "I'm right here, Eddie. I'm fine. The sheriff just wants to talk to us."

"If it's about that blasted festival, I have no interest in talking to him."

"I don't think you really have a choice, dear," she told him.

Still grumbling, Eddie followed his wife into the formal front room where Colin waited. Monroe and Hannah filed in behind him and took the seats Mrs. Conley suggested. Hannah noted that the mandolin was nowhere in sight.

"I'm sure you want to know why I'm here," the sheriff began. "But I think I'll let Monroe and Hannah tell you that. Hannah, will you start?"

For a moment Hannah was surprised, but she quickly realized the sheriff had chosen her as an impartial narrator. She cleared her throat and said, "Eddie, as we explained, Monroe and I were working at the library setting up a display for the upcoming bluegrass festival. What we didn't mention was what happened when we were unpacking a crate of instruments."

Hannah glanced at Colin for approval to proceed. He nodded.

She decided the best way to break the news was to do so simply. "In the crate, Monroe discovered what she believes to be your missing mandolin."

Eddie, who had appeared irritated, as though he just wanted this over with, suddenly sat up straight. "What did you say?"

"She said your mandolin was in the crate, Grandpa," Monroe answered, her voice cracking slightly as she repeated the words. "We found your mandolin."

"How would you recognize my mandolin?"

Monroe rolled her eyes and gestured at the photos of Eddie and the mandolin, which lined the walls and covered the mantel. "I wonder."

"The reason I'm here," Colin said, "is to confirm that this is indeed your mandolin." He nodded at Mrs. Conley, who reached beneath her chair to pull out the case.

Eddie stared at it as if he were seeing a ghost. "Is it all right?"

Monroe shook her head sadly. "You'll see. May I?" she asked the sheriff. When he agreed, she retrieved the case from her grandmother and walked across to kneel beside her grandfather. She placed the case on his lap and then sat back on her heels to watch him open it.

Hannah couldn't take her gaze off Eddie's face as he closed his eyes for a moment, probably trying to get his emotions under control. He took a long breath, then undid the clasps on the case. He lifted the lid, and his breath came out in a rush. He kept his head bowed as he reverently lifted the instrument and stroked his fingers across strings that had grown brittle and dry with age and lack of use.

Hannah saw him swallow hard. She couldn't begin to imagine what he must be feeling right now, to hold something so precious that he'd thought was lost forever. When he raised his head, his eyes were moist. "This mandolin was a gift from the greatest man ever to play bluegrass."

"Grandpa?"

Eddie glanced up at Monroe, who looked about ready to burst into tears. "What is it? What's wrong?"

Monroe was visibly struggling to speak, but she leaned forward and moved his fingers to the neck with the glued piece.

Eddie twisted his fingers to grasp hers and he smiled gently. "I know, darlin'. I felt it the minute I lifted it from the case. It's okay. I'm a little broken down myself now, but your nana still loves me. This mandolin is no less precious because of the break." His voice cracked. "I thought I'd never see it again."

Colin spoke up. "As happy as I am to have reunited you with your instrument, the fact is that I have a crime to investigate. So, I have to ask. Do you have any thoughts on who might have taken it all those years ago?"

Eddie hung his head. "I assume you know I blamed Ward Burton, our banjo player and lead vocalist." Colin nodded, and Eddie continued. "I didn't really think he took it. At least not when my temper settled. Whatever his problems were, Ward wouldn't have done that. He knew how much this mandolin meant to me because he was just as possessive about his banjo. My mandolin wasn't the only thing that went missing during the festival. If my mandolin was in the crate, was the money there too?"

"We have not located the money," Colin responded. "I assume it's long gone, but I instructed my deputy to search the remaining crates after she finishes taking statements from all the people who were in the library when the mandolin was discovered." The sheriff pulled out his notepad before speaking again. "Let's go through the list of people who would have had access the night it disappeared. Ladies, do you mind if we do this in private? I'll still need to speak to each of you some more."

"No problem." Hannah and Monroe left the room with Mrs. Conley, though Hannah couldn't imagine what else she would have to contribute.

Mrs. Conley invited them to the back porch for some lemonade and sandwiches. "I made chicken salad earlier."

"What, no sprinkle muffins?" Hannah teased a short time later as she helped spread chicken salad on crustless bread. "Maybe I should ask for the recipe and see if Jacob can duplicate it for the Hot Spot's young diners."

"If I'd have known you were coming, Hannah, I'd have whipped up a batch," Mrs. Conley replied with a touch of sass in her voice. "It's been way too long since you've been here with Monroe. And I apologize for not welcoming you properly before. I was surprised to see the sheriff, but that's no excuse for bad manners."

"Don't you worry at all, Mrs. Conley," Hannah said as she placed the sandwiches on a tray. "You've always made me feel welcome here. But I see you're not offering to share your recipe," she added with a laugh.

"Maybe I will if you call me Beverly instead of Mrs. Conley."

"Yes, ma'am," Hannah replied, grinning.

Monroe picked up the tray with the pitcher of lemonade and glasses. She pushed the screen door open with her foot and then held it with her back as Hannah and Beverly made their way out to the back porch with the food.

They settled in cushioned wicker chairs, and Monroe poured glasses of cold lemonade. When Hannah had hers, she picked up a sandwich half and eased back against the cushion. "It's so lovely and peaceful here."

The sun was high in the sky, but they were protected from its glare by the porch overhang. Birds sang in the trees, and a slight breeze kept the temperature comfortable. For the first time since they'd found the mandolin, Hannah felt her body relax. Monroe looked relieved.

Only Beverly seemed on edge, no doubt worried about the conversation taking place inside. "You know, I was a suspect initially."

"You were suspected of stealing the mandolin?" Monroe asked, her eyes wide.

Beverly nodded solemnly. "Eddie and I were going through a rough patch because I wanted him to stay home more. People heard us arguing, so when the sheriff was looking at suspects, he came to speak with me. Fortunately, I had an alibi."

"Who else did he suspect?"

"I couldn't say for sure, but I know he interviewed both our manager and promoter. That would have been Martin Lowe and Arthur White." She twisted her napkin in her lap. "I hope Sheriff Steele doesn't reopen old wounds."

Hannah wanted to reassure her, but she didn't know what to say. Maybe it would be better to try distraction. "Mrs. Taft asked Monroe and me to put together a bluegrass exhibit for the library, and I offered to do one at the Hot Spot too."

"You mean like the display you have of fire department memorabilia?"

"Exactly. I was thinking of asking my dad to make another case. What do you think?"

"I think you're trying to distract me from worrying about Eddie, and I love you for that." She smiled warmly at Hannah. "But I would love to have you share things at the Hot Spot. What did you have in mind?"

"That's the thing," Hannah said. "I know I like listening to bluegrass, and Liam and I visited the Bluegrass Hall of Fame last fall, but I feel like I don't know much about the Blackberry Valley festivals. Would it be too hard for you to talk about them, to help me understand what they were like?"

Beverly took a sip of her tea and set the glass back on its coaster. "I think I would like that very much, Hannah. Everyone remembers that the festival ended in a bitter feud, but it wasn't always that way." Beverly rested back in her chair and gave a sigh. "From the very first, the festival was a time of beautiful music, precious friendships, and adoring crowds of bluegrass fans. But before that, it was just Ward and Eddie. Two country boys who loved their bluegrass."

Blackberry Valley
June 1966

Blazing-hot sun beat down on the campgrounds outside Blackberry Valley as Eddie Conley mounted the make-shift stage. He and his partner, Ward Burton, had just finished hanging a huge banner over it that read, WELCOME TO BLACKBERRY VALLEY'S FIRST ANNUAL BLUEGRASS FESTIVAL. The sign had been made by his bride, Beverly.

Eddie mopped his brow with a handkerchief as he strode to the center of the stage with Beverly beside him. "Pinch me so I know this is real. When Ward and I dreamed up this crazy idea, I didn't believe it could ever happen. But people are actually lining up at the ticket booth."

"I believed it all along," Beverly declared as she linked her arm through his. "You and Ward were an incredible duo, but now that you've added Huck, Melvin, and Jasper to make a band, you're going to be unstoppable."

Eddie leaned over to kiss her. "You always believe in me more than I believe in myself. I guess that's because you love me."

"That's not the only reason. You only pay attention to playing your music, but I see what it does to the people who listen to it. When you're playing that mandolin, it's beautiful enough to make the angels cry."

Eddie ducked his head. "I'm not sure what I did to deserve you, Beverly Conley, but I thank God for you every day of my life."

"Are you two being goofy newlyweds again?" Ward Burton sauntered across the stage toward them. "People are coming to listen to us play, not watch you kiss."

"You're just jealous," Eddie retorted. "I told you to ask out Bev's friend Peggy."

"Aww shucks, Peggy won't even look at me."

"That's because she's shy, Ward," Beverly intervened. "I happen to know she'd say yes if you asked."

Ward's eyes lit up. "You think so?"

"I know so. Now you boys go change into your suits so you're ready to wow the crowd." Beverly gestured toward the lawn, where people were already spreading blankets and preparing to picnic as they listened to the concert.

An hour later, the newly formed Blackberry Mountain Boys took the stage to the sounds of whooping and hollering.

Ward stepped forward to welcome everyone and do the introductions. "Welcome to Blackberry Valley's first bluegrass festival. I'm Ward Burton, and this is my friend Eddie Conley. We grew up here, and many of you have been listening to us sing in back rooms since we were old enough to get in the door."

The crowd cheered.

Ward grinned and continued. "We know Eddie's pretty good on his mandolin." He paused while Eddie picked a sweet tune and the audience clapped. "And you've heard plenty from me. But we've added a few new members and have a whole new name. Please give it up for Huck on guitar, Melvin on Dobro, and Jasper on bass. Ladies and gents, I give you the Blackberry Mountain Boys!"

For hours the Blackberry Mountain Boys and other small acts played to a crowd that drank in every moment. Finally Ward took the microphone again. "Well, folks, that's about all we have for this year. We're going to wrap up with a song from me to a very special lady in the crowd." The band struck up the chords, and Ward crooned the lyrics to "Peggy-O."

When the last notes died away and the crowd reluctantly began to disperse, Eddie and Ward jumped down from the stage.

Beverly ran forward and leaped into Eddie's arms. "It was a smash. Everyone was saying they can't wait until your next festival. Oh, Eddie, it's going to be bigger and better every year," she proclaimed as he twirled her around.

Colin knocked on the frame of the screen door. "I need to speak with you now, Mrs. Conley." He glanced at his watch. "Hannah, I can give you a ride back to town after that. Monroe, if you need to pick up your car, you're welcome to come also."

Hannah nodded her assent, but she was distracted by how nervous Beverly seemed. Gone was the calm woman who had been happily relating tales of her past. Hannah supposed it was natural to be uneasy when being questioned by the sheriff, but Beverly looked more unnerved than that. Hannah recalled her words that she had once been a suspect. She'd laughed it off, but her appearance now belied that lighthearted mood. Hannah hated to even consider it, but was it possible Beverly was hiding something?

Chapter Six

It was midafternoon by the time Hannah made it to the Hot Spot. Colin had dropped them off at the library so Monroe could retrieve her car, and she'd immediately headed back to her grandparents' house. Hannah had intended to check in with Evangeline at the library, but the deputies had the building taped off while they continued their search for evidence. She glanced at the clock and decided there was just enough time to relax with a cup of tea before joining Jacob to begin dinner prep.

The kettle had whistled, and she was pouring water into her favorite mug when her phone rang with a call from Monroe. Hannah set the kettle down and picked up the call. "Hi, Monroe. Long time no talk."

"Hannah, I need your help!" Monroe sounded frantic. What could have caused such panic in the short time since they'd parted?

"Of course. What's wrong?"

"Everything," Monroe wailed. "By the time I got back to the house, it was bedlam. Grandpa Eddie has decided he doesn't trust the sheriff and intends to find out what happened to his mandolin himself. Nana's begging him to leave it alone, to let bygones be bygones and simply be happy he has his instrument back, but he won't hear of it."

"He seemed so peaceful about it before. What changed?"

"I don't know." Monroe's voice dropped. "He called Ward Burton. Whatever was said on that call sent him into a frenzy."

Hannah was struggling to imagine the gentle old man in such a state. "Maybe it's all just catching up with him, and he'll settle back down."

"That's not even the worst of it. Nana was really upset by his carrying on, and that's unlike her. She's always the calm one." Monroe let out a sigh. "At least she's resting quietly now. Hannah, please tell me you'll help figure this out. Liam said you're so great at solving mysteries."

Leaning back against the kitchen counter, Hannah swallowed hard. "That's a lot to ask, Monroe. I'm not a professional. I can't make promises that I can figure out what no one could when it happened. It's been fifty years. Isn't it enough that Sheriff Steele is reopening the case?"

Monroe was silent, but when she finally spoke again, Hannah could hear the strain choking her words. "I think they had a bad experience with the sheriff back in 1976. They know and trust you. If I tell them you're looking into it, maybe Grandpa will leave it alone. Hannah, they're too old for this kind of stress. I'm afraid it'll affect their health."

Hannah would have needed a heart of stone to refuse that plea. She'd solved mysteries for far less compelling reasons since her return to Blackberry Valley. This was personal. She closed her eyes and offered a prayer for guidance. "I can only promise that I'll investigate, Monroe. There's no guarantee I can solve it."

"You will. I know you will. Thank you, Hannah. I'll help however I can."

Hannah felt far less confident than her friend did, but she would do her best. "I'll need to brainstorm where to start. I'll get back to you when I have some ideas." She paused and let out a long, slow breath before adding, "You can tell your grandparents I'll try to find answers for them."

Half an hour later, Hannah waffled between concern and curiosity as she chopped the ends off asparagus spears for Jacob's hit Summer Salad. She wanted to know what had happened to the mandolin as much as anyone else, but she and Colin were the only ones expected to solve the mystery. For him, it was a job. For her, it was a promise to a friend, and two dear people were counting on her success. Even if that was an exaggeration, and Eddie and Beverly calmed down, Hannah knew they would have no peace of mind until they had answers.

"Hannah, do I need to remind you that you're wielding a very sharp knife?"

The head chef's voice cut through Hannah's thoughts, and she looked down at the mangled green spears on the cutting board. "I don't suppose you'd believe me if I said I was trying for a decorative touch."

Jacob shook his head. "No one expects their asparagus to be perfectly uniform, but they do prefer recognizable." He eyed her suspiciously. "This is how you get when you have a mystery to solve."

Hannah laughed, but even she could hear the tension in it.

Jacob's eyes grew wide. "You do have a new mystery. Let me guess—it has something to do with the long-lost mandolin everyone is talking about."

"Everyone's talking about it?" Hannah groaned. Of course they were. It was big news in the small town. Every person who had been in the library had witnessed it unfolding. And she had just promised to try to solve the mystery. Hannah pushed the chopped asparagus toward Jacob. "You'd better take over this part. Do we have any meat that needs pounding instead?"

By the time the Hot Spot opened, Hannah had managed to get herself on task. She might even have enjoyed the restaurant chatter about the mandolin if she hadn't been feeling the weight of her promise. At every table she visited, someone asked her about what happened. By the third time, she had a spiel down pat—Monroe had come across the mandolin in a storage box. When asked about Eddie's reaction, Hannah said he was happy to see his favorite instrument again. Any variation on those questions got a standard response about not being able to comment on an open police investigation. That drew sounds of approval, even though her patrons were disappointed that they weren't getting good firsthand gossip.

"Sheriff Steele ought to hire you as his spokesperson," Hot Spot hostess Elaine Wilby murmured when Hannah joined her. "You're really good at this."

"Thanks," Hannah replied. "I hope I'm as good at figuring out what happened." She filled Elaine in on Monroe's request. "I haven't had a chance to talk to Colin about seeing the files yet, but it's been fifty years and the police couldn't solve the case back then."

"Just because they didn't solve it doesn't mean they didn't have evidence or suspects. You and Colin will be looking at it with fresh eyes and the benefit of hindsight."

Hannah grinned. "I'm not the only one who's quick with answers. Thanks, Elaine. I think I'm just feeling a little overwhelmed to have a mystery to solve for a friend while also running a business, helping with the festival…" Her voice trailed off.

Elaine picked up. "And planning a wedding?"

With a nod, Hannah said, "Liam suggested we not stress over the plans, and I'm trying to just jot down notes when I get an idea, but there's so much to think about."

"And you have a lot of friends to help. Lean on us."

She gave Elaine a quick hug. "Thank you. And you're right about the suspects. I learned about a few today. I'll see Colin at our festival committee meeting tomorrow morning, so I'll ask to see the old case files then."

"See, you can do it." Elaine smiled and held out a trio of menus. "You might want to take a peek at who just came in looking for a table."

Hannah swung around, and the tension drained from her body immediately as she saw Liam, firefighter Colt Walker, and Marshall talking in the doorway.

Liam flashed her a grin. "We heard there was some smashed asparagus soup on the menu tonight."

Hannah burst out laughing. "Okay, Jacob is fired. Which one of you did he squeal to?" She pretended to glare at Marshall. "Weren't you here earlier, working on his festival menu?"

Marshall held up his hands in mock surrender. "The soup is great. I just asked what inspired it."

Hannah was still laughing as she led them to a table, and she had to admit that felt much better than stewing in her anxiety. "Since you already know the special, I'll send Raquel over to take the rest of your orders. I hope you enjoy the soup."

She walked away and headed through the swinging doors into the kitchen. "Hey, Jacob. I have two hungry firefighters and a food critic who came in for your soup special." She coughed lightly.

Jacob flipped a burger on the grill and wiped his hands on his apron. "What can I say? When life gives you mangled asparagus, make soup."

Still wearing a wide grin on her face, Hannah reentered the dining room. Every single night she was reminded of how much she loved living in Blackberry Valley and running the Hot Spot with people who filled her life with joy.

Later, Liam approached her at the hostess stand. "I was hoping I might convince you to go for a moonlight stroll with me after work. I'll even help with cleanup."

"That's an offer I'd be a fool to pass up."

"The help with cleanup, or the walk?" Liam quipped.

"Either. Both." Hannah leaned in for a quick kiss. "Honestly, it feels like weeks ago that we were having coffee this morning. A moonlight walk with you is just what I need to end the day."

True to his word, Liam stayed until the restaurant emptied of diners, then helped make short work of the cleanup. Once they were finished, Hannah grabbed a light jacket. After she let everyone out and locked up, she and Liam headed along Main Street. The June night was clear and warm with only a quarter moon to light their way.

As they strolled along, Hannah tried to let the calm of the evening wash over her, but it wasn't working.

"Want to tell me what's wrong?" Liam asked, startling her out of her reverie.

"How do you know something is?"

Liam stopped and drew her against his side. "I know you. You get this distracted look when you're pondering clues, but you tighten your shoulders when you're worried. Tonight, you've been doing both."

Hannah leaned into him. "You're right." She slipped her hand into his, and they began walking again. "Monroe called me this afternoon. She was desperate because her grandfather has decided to solve the mystery on his own, and her grandmother was extremely upset."

"I'm sure it's rough on them to have everything brought back into the light after all these years."

"That's what's confusing me. At first Eddie was just glad to have his mandolin back. Beverly was happy too—at least until Colin took her to another room for questioning. But Monroe said she went into a panic when Eddie said he was going to investigate on his own."

"Could something have come up during Colin's interviews with them?"

"I hadn't considered that, but it makes sense since they both seemed okay before they spoke with him. They were also in shock though, so maybe it was the shock wearing off too."

"But you're still worried?" Liam guessed.

Hannah nodded.

"Are you worried that one of the Conleys might have been hiding something all these years?"

"Beverly told us she'd been a suspect during the first investigation, but that she had an alibi." Hannah leaned back and raised her face to the moon, sighing as she felt the thoughts that had been plaguing her all evening come into focus. "Liam, what if her alibi wasn't true? Monroe asked me to investigate the case, but what if I find something that hurts the family even more?"

Chapter Seven

Hannah rose early on Saturday morning, feeling no more settled than she had the night before. She was eager to do a little research before her festival committee meeting at nine, though she was still afraid of what she might find. What she really needed was to pray about this, so she brewed a cup of coffee to sip while reading her morning devotion.

She opened the book. Today's reading was from Paul's letters to the Colossians. "*Therefore, as God's chosen people, holy and dearly loved, clothe yourselves with compassion, kindness, humility, gentleness and patience. Bear with each other and forgive one another if any of you has a grievance against someone. Forgive as the Lord forgave you.*"

Hannah leaned back against her chair. It never ceased to amaze her how timely her devotions could be. This chapter provided a good lesson to keep in mind as she focused on solving the mystery.

The time spent reading Scripture had settled her mind. God's will would be done, and if that meant uncovering unpleasant truths, that was still His will. She prayed that if her discoveries reopened old wounds the result would be forgiveness and healing.

The next step became clear. Hannah needed to speak privately with Beverly and ask her if she was afraid of something coming to light.

After pouring a second cup of coffee, Hannah settled down at the table with her laptop. She would do some research, gather information, then present it to Beverly and gauge her reaction.

Hannah did a search for *missing mandolin Blackberry Valley bluegrass festival.*

The first set of search results were all about the previous day's discovery. News certainly traveled fast. She scanned the articles to see if there had been any developments overnight, but the information was pretty basic—just the official statement from the Blackberry Valley Sheriff's Department and quotes from a number of people who had been volunteering at the library.

Hannah scrolled past the current entries until the results jumped back decades. There was a series of articles from *The Blackberry Valley Chronicle*, but when she tried to read one, she discovered the link was broken. Hannah took note of the byline and decided to make time to stop by the newspaper office to look at the actual articles. By the time she'd put a reminder in her phone, it was time to head over to her committee meeting.

Since the library was still off-limits, the meeting had been moved, but it was only a short walk from her apartment above the Hot Spot to the new location at town hall. As Hannah strolled along the sidewalk in the pleasantly warm morning sunlight, she met up with other community members who were headed in the same direction. As soon as the festival had been announced, the local business owners had formed a committee—along with the sheriff's department and the fire department—to make certain that Blackberry Valley would be prepared to host the influx of tourists and musicians. The goal was to offer them a safe and fun event that would also benefit the valley's small businesses.

There was always a lot of excited chatter when they gathered, but this morning the crowd buzzed about the discovery of the mandolin. Everyone had questions for Hannah, but she managed to defer most of them to Colin. As the committee members settled around a large conference table in the sunlit room, the sheriff conferred with Lacy's husband, Neil Minyard, who'd been chosen as committee chair. Neil soon called the meeting to order and announced that the first order of business had been changed to a report from Sheriff Steele.

Colin pushed back his chair and stood so everyone could see him. "I'm here to update you on the safety plan for the festival, but I understand you are all curious about yesterday's developments, so let me address them first." He cleared his throat and began. "As you might have heard..." He paused as chuckles rippled around the table. "Eddie Conley's mandolin, which went missing on the closing night of the 1976 festival, mysteriously appeared in the library yesterday. I can confirm that it is the same mandolin that went missing. I'm sure you all have questions, but this is an active investigation, so that is all I have to say about it at this time. I'll update you as I am able, since I recognize that there may be related concerns about how this news and the investigation might impact the festival."

"I'm betting the news will bring more gawkers to town," grumbled Earl Tate, the manager of what could only be termed a junk shop.

"I expect you're right about that, Earl," Colin replied. "All the more reason to move on to talking about our security preparations.

This morning I spoke to the festival promoter about hiring additional security given the news. He was agreeable."

"I guess he's seeing more dollar signs based on this discovery," Zane Forrest commented. "Earl, those 'gawkers' will all need a place to stay and food to eat. I'm sure they'll be looking for trinkets to remember the trip as well, so we'll all benefit."

Earl mumbled another grumpy comment, but Evangeline cut him off.

"Oh, hush, Earl. You're turning into as much of a curmudgeon as your father was." There were more than a few puzzled expressions around the table, so she continued. "Earl is just the latest in a line of Tates opposing anything that might bring tourists and their money to town. As if we don't all benefit when people visit."

Hannah could hear some whispering on her side of the table. The words weren't clear, but as she strained, she thought she heard someone hinting that Earl's father himself might have had something to do with the mandolin going missing. She glanced at Colin, but he was deep in conversation with Neil across the room and didn't seem to have heard.

Colin raised his voice to address the room again. "That's really all for now. I'll have updates to the security plan by early next week. If no one has any other questions, I'll turn it back over to our chairman."

Neil called for the committee reports. Everyone settled down to business, though there was an undercurrent of energy that hadn't been present at their previous meetings. The Garden Club and Decorations Committee presented their report on a plan to install hanging baskets of Kentucky bluegrass with an assortment of native flowers on all the lampposts along Main Street. Welcome banners had been commissioned to be stretched across intersections at both ends of town. The reports droned on, and though Hannah was usually thrilled to be a part of the local business community, today she was itching to get back to her own investigation.

Eventually, the meeting wound to a close, and everyone rose to stretch. Hannah made her way over to talk to Evangeline, who chatted with Seeds of Joy owner Shannon Radcliff. Hannah waited for a break in the conversation, then addressed Evangeline. "I heard you talking about Earl Tate's father. No one really believed he stole the mandolin, did they?"

The two women exchanged a glance. "No one ever accused him of anything," Evangeline said carefully. "But he was so grumpy that he made Earl look like a welcome committee. He didn't like people tromping across his property. He tried to force a cancellation of the festival in '76, and when that didn't work, he called the sheriff's office every night, complaining that the festival musicians were in violation of some noise ordinance."

"It gave us a reprieve," Shannon said with a laugh. "Usually he was calling to complain about the teenagers hanging out at the campgrounds."

"He sounds like an unhappy man," Hannah commented, trying not to badmouth someone she'd never met.

"People said he was born an old codger." Shannon laughed. "But nobody let him get to them. He was acknowledged and accepted around town for who he was—a colorful character."

Hannah knew exactly what they meant. Most towns had a person or two who fit that description, and as long as they didn't hurt anyone, no one paid them much mind. The question was, though, had Earl's father taken action? Had he seen his complaints falling on deaf ears and taken matters—or a mandolin—into his own hands?

She saw Colin heading toward the door, so she excused herself and hurried to catch up with him. "Sheriff?"

He turned and waited for her to reach him. "Hi, Hannah. I have to get back to the station. Did you need something?"

"More like I wanted to share something. It's probably nothing important, but I'll leave that for you to decide."

"I appreciate that. What is it?"

"Let's wait until we get outside. I'll walk with you."

"Well, now you've got me curious."

Hannah chuckled but kept walking. Once they were clear of the entrance and had no one within earshot, she spoke. "I'm not trying to be mysterious. It's more that I don't want to spread unfounded gossip."

"Understood."

"It's something I overheard at the meeting. You were talking to Neil, so I don't think you heard."

"The remarks about Earl's father?"

Hannah let out an exasperated sigh. "I should have known you were listening."

The sheriff smiled. "I heard the initial comments, but not whatever Evangeline and Shannon told you after."

So he'd also noticed her approach them. No moss ever grew on Sheriff Steele. "I asked if they really thought he would have taken the mandolin." She proceeded to relay her conversation. "But as I'm telling you this, I'm thinking it doesn't make much sense to consider him a suspect. He might have broken the mandolin in a flash of anger, but why would he have glued it back together and returned it?"

"Good question. I'm not inclined to consider Earl's father a suspect, but I've also learned not to rule out anyone too quickly. How's that?"

"I trust what you do with any information I bring you. You're the sheriff."

He laughed heartily. "I appreciate the compliment, Hannah. Now what else are you dying to ask me?"

Hannah joined his laughter. "You know me a bit too well. I was just wondering if you'd had a chance to look at the old case files yet?"

"No, I was tied up at the library for hours yesterday. No sign of the money anywhere, in case you're wondering. Like I said before, it was probably spent decades ago. I'm going to go check in at the library now and then head over to the station. Once I've gone over the files, I'll probably be able to let you look at them." He chuckled at her expression. "I knew you wouldn't like me adding the word 'probably,' but I'm officially reopening the investigation. The theft of the mandolin alone makes the crime a felony. In Kentucky that means there is no statute of limitations. I can't make any promises about what I can share with you until I know what I'm dealing with."

"I understand. I'll wait patiently."

Colin snorted. "We both know you won't do that."

"Okay, I'll *try* to wait patiently. I'll see what else I can find in the meantime." Hannah was saved from making any more promises when her phone buzzed. Elaine's name flashed on the display, so Hannah decided she'd better take it. She said a quick goodbye to Colin, then stopped to answer her call. "Good morning, Elaine."

"Hi, Hannah. Sorry to bother you. I know you had a meeting, but I wanted to give you a heads-up. We just got a reservation for a party of twenty for tonight."

"Twenty?" Hannah's jaw dropped. They'd hosted large groups before, but guests usually reserved far in advance for special occasions. "Who is it?"

"The production team that's in town to set up for the festival. Apparently Marshall had something on his site recommending the Hot Spot as *the* place in town for great food and conversation."

"Remind me to give Marshall an extra slice of pie along with my thanks. How do our other reservations look? Can we handle such a big party?"

"It'll be tight, but if everyone's on board, we can manage."

"Thanks, Elaine. I'll call Jacob. I wonder if Raquel knows."

"She does, and she's told Dylan. Raquel was the one who tipped me off to check the online reservations. She didn't want to disturb you in your meeting. Hope it went well."

Hannah counted herself blessed to have such a dedicated staff that they often checked in outside of work hours. "It did. Naturally the mandolin was the big topic of conversation. We're expecting to get more visitors once this news spreads. But Sheriff Steele has it all under control."

"Of course he does."

"I'm heading back to the restaurant now. I'll get right to work prepping as soon as I reach Jacob."

"See you soon. I'll be in early myself," Elaine replied.

Hannah called and relayed the information to Jacob, then hurried home to get ready for work. It seemed that her sleuthing would be delayed again, but the night sounded exciting.

Chapter Eight

Hannah was back to mashing asparagus when Jacob walked into the kitchen an hour later. She grinned when she caught him staring at her cutting board. "The soup was such a smash hit last night that I thought we could go for an encore."

Jacob groaned at her pun, but agreed with the menu plan. He donned an apron, then he and Hannah got to work prepping to feed a larger-than-normal Saturday crowd. As they worked together, Hannah filled him in on her morning committee meeting.

"Do you really think the discovery of the mandolin will bring more people to the festival?" Jacob asked. "I'm not sure I'd bother to come all the way here for an instrument that isn't going to be displayed or even played. It's not, right?"

"That's a good question," Hannah replied as she removed her apron and prepared to help in the dining room. "According to Monroe, Eddie adamantly refuses to participate. She said he hasn't performed publicly since the Blackberry Mountain Boys broke up. But I wonder if finding his mandolin will change that."

"Now *that* would bring a crowd," Jacob said as he worked a crust for a summer vegetable pie that had proven popular.

Hannah couldn't shake that vision as she bustled around the dining room with Elaine, Raquel, and Dylan, setting places and making sure everything was ready to open. She only realized she was humming "Wayfaring Stranger" when she caught Dylan staring. "What?"

He ducked his head. "My dad loved that song. He used to hum it just like you are."

"Oh, Dylan. I'm sorry." Dylan's father had passed away suddenly some years before.

"It's okay." He smiled at Hannah. "It's a happy memory. He would have been excited about this festival. I'm going to bring my mom and sisters."

"You're such a good young man. Your dad would be very proud of you." Hannah knew it was time to change the conversation when she saw tears welling in his eyes. "Will you come help me put some tables together?"

The restaurant opened, and before long Hannah was too busy to think about anything other than the diners who needed to be served. She filled in wherever necessary when the crowd peaked, and breathed a sigh of relief when satiated diners finished their meals and vacated their tables, making room for others.

One of the tables near the front was occupied by two people Hannah didn't know. She made her way through the crowd to introduce herself. "Hello, I'm the Hot Spot's owner, Hannah Prentiss. I don't think I've seen you here before, so I wanted to come greet you myself."

The man looked up from his menu. "Hello, Hannah. Thank you for the welcome. I'm Harrison White, and this is my grandmother, Ellie. You wouldn't know us because we're in town for the festival."

Hannah might not know the faces, but she knew the name. "Wasn't a White the promoter of the original Blackberry Valley Bluegrass Festival?"

"I'm impressed that you know that. Yes, my grandfather, Arthur White, was the original promoter. The festival was his brainchild."

"And is reviving it your brainchild, Mr. White?"

"Harry, please. Yes, after my grandfather passed, Grandmother and I were talking about how time flies and how it had been almost fifty years since the last festival. That's what put the idea in my head. It felt like time to clean the tarnish and revive a wonderful tradition."

Hannah fought to hide her smile. Harry sure had a promoter's gift of gab. "Well, we are certainly excited that you decided to do so. I'm part of the festival committee, which is why I knew your grandfather's name. On behalf of all of us, thank you." Hannah turned to Ellie White. "Were you here for the original festivals with your husband, Mrs. White?"

The woman managed a gracious smile, but Hannah didn't miss a slight look of unease.

"Ellie, please. And yes, I was. Arthur and I were newlyweds during the first festival. I loved returning to Blackberry Valley every year, so when Harrison decided to revive the festival, I knew I had to join him. I love your restaurant. As I recall, this was the firehouse back then, was it not?"

"You have a wonderful memory. Yes, it was. The fire department moved into a modern building, and I renovated this one. It was a longtime dream of mine to open my own restaurant."

"Well, by all appearances, you've created something very special here, Hannah."

"Thank you," Hannah replied.

Suddenly, Harry greeted a woman who had approached the table. "Mrs. Lowe, hello."

Ellie stood to hug the newcomer. "Shelby, how good it is to see you. Harry didn't tell me you were coming."

"He didn't know. I really didn't decide until the last minute."

Hannah waited quietly while they greeted each other, but her thoughts whirred. She remembered the name Lowe too. Martin Lowe had been the manager of the Blackberry Mountain Boys and another early suspect in the missing mandolin case. She didn't see a man with Shelby. Was he still alive?

Ellie turned back. "Hannah, let me introduce a dear friend. Shelby and I used to spend our days and evenings together while our husbands worked around the clock. We haven't seen each other in years. Shelby, Hannah owns this charming restaurant. Remember it used to be a firehouse when we were here?"

Shelby greeted Hannah. "Lovely to meet you. I've heard nothing but good things about you and your restaurant."

"I'm glad," Hannah said. "How did you hear about us?"

"I was lucky there was a cancellation at Sally's Bed and Breakfast, and I was able to get a room. Amelia Jacobsen, the owner, told me this was the place to come for dinner. That you would make me feel welcome." She glanced around the room. "Seems like everyone got the same recommendation."

Hannah's heart overflowed with joy at the words. Seeing her restaurant filled with so many happy people was the fruition of her dearest dream. "Thank you so much. Can I find you a table, or will you be joining the Whites?"

"Please join us, Shelby," Ellie urged. "Once the production team arrives, Harry will abandon me, so we'll have time to catch up."

When Shelby agreed, Hannah signaled to Dylan to bring another place setting. While he did, she recited the specials. "Raquel will be by momentarily to take your orders. I'll be back to check in later, but please wave me down if you need anything."

Hannah had time to check in with a few of her regulars before a group of people at the hostess stand caught her attention. The production team had arrived. Hannah hastened over to give Elaine a hand getting them seated and handing out menus. She introduced herself and repeated her welcome as a member of the festival committee.

The smiling men and women returned her greeting.

Recognizing that they were cheerful but tired and hungry after a long day of work, Hannah cut through the chitchat. "I'm sure you're all starving. Your waitress will be right with you. If there are any special diets or requests, just let her know and we'll be happy to accommodate. I hope you enjoy your meal."

Hannah left them and headed into the kitchen to alert Jacob. Her chef also looked tired but content. "Do you need help with anything back here?"

Jacob tossed wings in his famous Inferno sauce. "Raquel just left with an order for table ten, but there was more than she could carry."

"On it." Hannah took the plates he indicated and loaded them onto a tray, then backed through the swinging door with it. She wound her way through the tables and set the tray down beside the one Raquel had brought out.

Hannah was exhausted but grateful by the time she finally began to switch off the Hot Spot's lights. They'd had an overflowing Saturday house, a mix of regulars along with the festival's production team.

The crowd had kept her hopping all night, and the bluegrass music on the sound system kept her energized. Until now. The physical fatigue that suddenly swamped her was a good feeling, but nagging concerns about the mandolin mystery came creeping back in the silence that filled the restaurant. She really hoped she could find answers quickly so the mystery wasn't hanging over the festival's opening.

She flicked the last switch and had just started for the stairs when her phone buzzed. The screen lit up with a text from *Liam "My Fiancé!" Berthold*, and Hannah's heart gave a kick as she read his message. He hadn't changed his contact name—a charming habit of his—in a while, but she was fine with that. *My fiancé* had a nice ring.

Meet me out back?

Hannah's heart lifted and her fatigue evaporated as she texted her reply. On my way.

She unlocked the rear door and slipped out, and there he was, leaning against his Jeep and wearing his heart-stopping smile. As she closed the door behind her, he straightened and opened his arms.

Hannah walked right into them and sighed softly as they closed around her. "How did you know I needed to see you?"

She could feel his whole body relax. "Maybe I'm the one who needed to see you."

Hannah leaned back so she could study his face. "Another rough day?"

"Not really. You were worried last night, so I wanted to see how you are tonight."

"I'm still concerned," she said as he took her hand and started to walk along the street. "But we had such a great night at the Hot Spot." She told him about her conversation with Harry, Ellie, and Shelby and how the whole production team had come for a late dinner based on Marshall's recommendation.

"That's great, Hannah. And Colin told me the committee meeting went well this morning."

"It did, but it would have been better if you'd been there."

He squeezed her hand in reply. "I had an inspection scheduled that couldn't be moved. I imagine the mandolin was a hot topic of conversation."

"Yes, but Earl kind of took over with his complaints. Did you know his father? I don't remember him, but some of the business owners were saying that he was always trying to shut the old festival down."

"I met him once or twice. He and his son were a pair of pack rats, and my dad got called out a few times with complaints of safety violations. I went with him once. That was enough. The place made quite an impression on a kid who liked to collect things. After that day, I learned the benefits of culling and storing."

Hannah laughed at the image of a young, impressionable Liam. "Well I'm glad for whatever made you and your dad keep all those bluegrass magazines so well protected in storage. I feel like I have more background going into this investigation because of all the articles I read when I was looking for Chuck."

"Then what's got you down?"

"I tried doing some research today and had a chat with Colin about the files—which he agreed to consider sharing with me after he reviews them. But honestly, I don't know where to start other than reading newspaper articles."

"I had an idea about that," Liam said. "I asked my grandfather if he knew anything. He said he worked the fire out at the festival."

"There was a fire?"

"Apparently on that last night, there was also a fire in the ticket booth. Gramps had some interesting theories about it, but it would be better if you heard them from him."

Hannah's mood immediately perked up. "Do you think he'd like to come to dinner at my dad's house tomorrow? We could pick him up after church."

"I'm sure he'd love it. I'll call in the morning and let you know."

"Thanks, Liam."

Liam slowed as they approached the streetlight.

When Hannah glanced at him, she saw a smile on his face. "What?"

"I was just thinking of when we took another walk along this street back in November."

Hannah laughed. "You mean when you asked me out on a date, and I thought you just wanted to go for a walk?"

Liam's smile broadened as he stopped. "Best walk of my life, and here we are still walking together all these months later." Leaning down, he rested his forehead against hers. "Hannah, I want to still be walking by your side when we're old and gray and have been married for fifty years. Deal?"

Hannah beamed at him. "Deal, but let's make it sixty years. I love you."

"And I love you," Liam murmured as he kissed her.

Hannah awoke in a much brighter mood on Sunday morning. She yawned and stretched before heading to the kitchen for coffee. Her laptop beckoned, so she decided to read a little about the fire before church, so she'd have a better idea of what to ask Patrick Berthold.

Within seconds, *fire at Blackberry Valley bluegrass festival* brought up a series of articles. There were even a few photos of the aftermath. Hannah zoomed in on one of them. Was she imagining it, or were there charred bills on the ground? It would make sense that money could have burned since presumably a ticket booth would hold cash, but did this fire have something to do with the missing money? Had it possibly burned up?

She was out of time to research more, so Hannah headed to her closet to select a light floral dress for church. She chose beige sandals and a matching purse to complete the outfit. After the service, she and Liam planned to drive straight to Clarkston Commons, the retirement center near Cave City where Patrick lived, so they were carpooling. Once she was ready, Hannah rinsed out her coffee mug and headed downstairs to wait for him.

Her heart lifted as the familiar blue Jeep turned the corner. Hannah was struck with the conviction that she would always feel this way when she saw Liam. Her parents had been happily married for decades before her mom died. Hannah wanted that same happiness for her life with Liam, so in that moment, she vowed that she would work every day at their marriage, making the effort to never take the man she loved for granted. And that started right now.

Liam parked the Jeep and came around to hold the door for her. Before she climbed in, she kissed him. "Thank you for being you."

Liam gave her a quizzical look. "Who else would I be?"

She laughed. "No one. You're perfect just being you."

Liam grinned. "I have no idea what I did to deserve this greeting, but I'll take it."

They arrived at Grace Community Church with time to spare. Hannah and Liam joined her father and uncle in their regular pew. She spotted Monroe with her grandmother, and in the moment their eyes met, Hannah's peace fled. Monroe looked even more stressed than she'd sounded on the phone Friday night, and Hannah felt guilty for not touching base with her yesterday. She made a mental note to suggest that Lacy invite Monroe and Beverly for Puzzle Night. They could both probably use some relaxing social time.

Hannah settled in between Liam and her father, offering a grateful prayer that God had gifted her the love of two strong, godly men. The opening hymn began, and she forced herself to set her worries aside and focus her attention where it belonged. When Pastor Bob began to preach a message of peace and hope from Romans 5, Hannah realized how it connected with her own reading from Colossians. She could only pray that when this mystery was solved, there would be forgiveness and peace.

As soon as church services ended, Liam drove them to Cave City. Patrick was waiting for them.

"Hannah!" Liam's grandfather pulled her into a hug. "I hope my grandson has been treating you well."

"Of course he has," Hannah replied with a wink at Liam. "You and his parents raised him right."

While Liam got his grandfather settled in the front seat beside him, Hannah climbed into the back and quickly texted Lacy about inviting Monroe and Beverly to Puzzle Night. Lacy immediately replied with a thumbs-up, so Hannah put her phone away and leaned forward to talk with Patrick.

"So what have you been up to since I saw you last?" Although she was dying to question him about the fire, her parents had raised her right, too, and she knew better than to dive straight into that as if she had no other reason for coming out to see him. She honestly loved Liam's grandfather and wanted to hear about his days.

"I've been gardening."

Hannah's jaw dropped. "Did I hear that right?"

Patrick nodded. "One of the 4-H camps has been sending young people out to establish a community garden at Clarkston Commons. Last night, we had salad with our home-grown greens, carrots, and even tomatoes."

"I'm impressed."

"You should be." Patrick grinned. "Who would have ever guessed this old fireman could have such a green thumb? Maybe one of these days I'll be supplying your restaurant too." He winked at Hannah. "I've been playing some bluegrass too. A bus will bring us to the festival next weekend. More than a few of us have fond memories of the old festival, so the staff dug up some instruments for us, and we've been having our own little jam sessions in the evening."

"You've been a busy man."

"Helps keep me young."

Hannah hoped she had half his energy and zest for life when she reached his age. "What instrument are you playing?"

"I decided to try the banjo. Some of my friends are playing bass and guitar. None of us will win any awards, but we're having fun."

Patrick entertained them with more of his stories until they arrived at the house Hannah had grown up in. Now her father lived there with her uncle Gordon and a border terrier named Zeus, who came running to greet them now, barking happily. The two widowers enjoyed each other's company and had developed numerous interests to keep them busy. They'd honed their skills with the grill, so Hannah wasn't a bit surprised when her father came around the side of the house to greet them. He wore his cookout apron and held tongs, but he wrapped her in a bear hug anyway. "There's my girl."

Hannah laughed. "The same one who sat beside you in church this morning."

Her father turned to greet Liam's grandfather. "Patrick, it's been too long. I'm glad you could join us. You've got to try this new rib recipe Gordon and I have been working on."

Liam and Hannah fell back as Dad and Patrick headed to the yard. "Do you want to sit out back with the men or join me in the kitchen?" Hannah asked him. "I promised Dad I would whip up a strawberry shortcake for dessert if he picked up the berries. I want to set them macerating while we eat."

Her fiancé gave her a quizzical look. "You marinate berries? Like you would meat?"

Hannah smiled. "*Macerate*, not marinate. It's a cooking term. You cut up the berries and mix them with sugar, then let them sit to pull out the juices. We'll have them later with cake and whipped cream."

Liam's expression eased. "That sounds much more appealing. Even so, maybe I'll stay with you to make sure you don't slip in any Worcestershire sauce from the rib marinade."

They headed straight to the kitchen. Hannah found the basket of berries and began to wash them. After Liam patted them dry, she pulled out the cutting board, but Liam rested his hand on hers before she could grab the knife.

"You sure you should be doing this part? I'll be happy to cut them for you. I hear you've been having a hard time managing knives lately."

Hannah burst into laughter. "I really am going to have to have a chat with Jacob about sharing kitchen stories." She pulled out an extra cutting board and two knives. "Let's see your skills."

They chatted easily as they worked, and once the berries were set, Hannah called to her father to see if he needed anything.

"Gordon says he made a salad earlier, and there's also potato salad in the refrigerator if you could bring that out."

Liam and Hannah carried everything to the picnic table on the patio. "You men are turning into quite the gourmet chefs," he said.

"A man's got to eat anyway. He might as well eat well," Uncle Gordon rejoined.

Uncle Gordon and Dad ferried the platter of ribs to the table. Once they had taken their places and filled their plates, they bowed their heads and Patrick led them in a blessing.

Hannah bided her time as everyone enjoyed their meal, but when the conversation hit a lull, she turned to Patrick. "Liam told me you fought a fire out at the festival grounds in '76. That was the first I heard of any fire. I read some articles this morning, but I'd love to hear about your experience if you're willing to talk about it."

"On another case, are you?" Patrick patted his full belly and leaned back in his chair. "Sure. It was the last night of the festival.

We rushed out there as soon as the call came in. We feared the worst given the size of the crowd, so it was a relief to find it confined to the ticket booth. Some people at the festival had jumped into action and thrown melted ice from their coolers on the flames. That kept the fire from spreading until we got there and put it out."

"I saw a photo online of the ticket booth after the fire was out. It looked like there was charred money. Was I seeing that right?" Hannah asked.

Patrick nodded. "I'm not sure why whoever was working the booth didn't take the money with them when they fled the fire, but there were piles of burned bills."

"Is it possible that the money was never stolen? That it all just burned up?"

"No. There wasn't enough ash for that."

"Did anyone see how the fire started?"

Patrick shook his head. "The crowd was huge, so anyone could have dropped a match and kept going. With all that paper from the tickets and the money—well, it was bound to go up."

"That sounds either careless or intentional."

"Oh, it was arson, pure and simple. People who aren't trying to start fires make sure their lit matches are out before they toss them."

"But who would want to do that?" Hannah couldn't wrap her mind around it.

Patrick met her gaze squarely. "Who would want to steal the money and Eddie Conley's mandolin? Mark my words, Hannah. When you find the thief, you'll find the arsonist too."

Chapter Nine

Early Monday morning, Hannah headed over to the *Chronicle* with Patrick's words about arson still ringing in her head. Jack Delaney, the newspaper's editor-in-chief, was often at his desk long before the office officially opened. She was hoping he would have time to let her access the old newspaper archives. Armed with Patrick's information, she was particularly eager to read any articles about the theft and fire.

Jack had been a big help on some previous cases, and he loved his morning coffee, so she stopped by Jump Start Coffee on her way and picked up his favorite brew, along with a scone in case he'd forgotten to eat breakfast that morning. The shop was bustling even at this early hour, so she placed her order and had a quick chat with Zane, who pointed out his cookie arrangement. The display case included an array of musical instrument-shaped cookies. Hannah sent a photo to Jacob, asking if he wanted to talk to his brother about including them on the dessert menu. They'd be a fun addition to a bowl of ice cream or fresh fruit.

When Hannah knocked on the front door, Jack was already at his desk as she'd suspected he might be. He rose and greeted her with a suspicious smile. "Good morning, Hannah. I see you come with bribes. What can I help you with today?"

"Not bribes. It's not a crime to want to share morning coffee with a friend, is it?"

"Certainly not, but when that friend comes in at the crack of dawn on her day off, one does wonder," he replied in a teasing tone. "Come on back to my office."

Hannah set Jack's coffee and scone down in front of him and then settled in the seat across from his desk. "You're right, of course. I do have an ulterior motive for stopping by. But I haven't had coffee yet, so I thought we could enjoy it while we talk. If you're not too busy." She took a sip of her coffee, then set the cup down on the edge of his desk in front of her.

"I'm guessing this has something to do with the missing mandolin," Jack said as he sat back down and broke off a bite of scone.

"Is anyone in this town talking about anything else this week?"

"True. How about a fair trade? You can ask me your questions, and then you give me an exclusive."

Hannah rested her chin in her hand and mulled over how to answer. "That doesn't seem like much of a bargain for you because everyone witnessed what I know. Monroe and I found the mandolin when we were unpacking a crate to set up for a festival exhibit. Eddie Conley did confirm it's his, but that's about all anyone knows at this point."

"But you're not satisfied with that, right?"

She gave him a look. "You know me well. Sheriff Steele is investigating, but Monroe Taylor asked me to see what I could find out too. That's why I'm here. I was searching for information online and found a series of *Chronicle* articles by Maureen Hughes. I couldn't access them online, so I was hoping I could read them from your archives."

Jack assessed her, his eyes sharp. "Any chance Monroe would talk to me? You can certainly view our archives, but it would be nice to have an interview with her to run along with the headline news."

"I'll call and ask." Hannah grinned. "At a more reasonable hour."

"Good enough." He gulped some coffee, then turned to his computer and hit some keys. "Hmm." He typed something else and then frowned as he looked up at Hannah. "I see the name, but it looks like the articles were never scanned and uploaded. Do you have the exact dates of Maureen's articles?"

Hannah reached to pull her notebook from her tote bag. "It was June to July of 1976."

Jack typed in the information, and his frown deepened. "Those entire issues seem to be missing from the online archives."

Hannah struggled to restrain her immediate instinct to suspect something nefarious. "Is there a reasonable explanation for why that might happen?"

Jack shrugged. "Maybe. There's only one way to find out. Are you game for a trek to the basement?"

She was glad she'd worn sneakers instead of sandals. "Let's do it."

Jack reached into his side desk drawer and withdrew a heavy key chain.

Hannah finished her coffee and tossed the cup in the trash before following him down the hallway.

Jack unlocked a door, then flicked a light switch at the top of the stairs, and they headed down into the dimly lit basement. The *Chronicle* building was old, but it had obviously been well-maintained over the years, so the trip into storage wasn't as bad as it sounded. Cement covered the brick-lined walls, providing protection from leaks for the rows upon rows of metal shelving units of clearly labeled, heavy-duty bins.

After taking a moment to get his bearings, Jack led her down a narrow corridor between two sets of racks. "The dates we want should be at the end of this row."

Hannah observed the dates on the nearest bin—NOVEMBER 1–15, 1976. The next one down was labeled the same way but for October 16 through the end of the month. She mentally counted backward. If there were two bins per month, the issues they wanted should be the ninth and tenth ones, but when she counted that far ahead, she saw only an empty space.

Jack stood in front of the shelves with his hands on his hips and a frown on his face. "Everything from June is missing. Are you sure of those dates?"

"I am. The first article was a preview of opening night of the 1976 festival. There seemed to be several more articles after that."

Jack opened the bin labeled AUGUST and peered inside. "These editions are definitely from August of 1976." He moved down the row and opened the ones marked MAY. Likewise, they correctly contained the May newspapers. "Something's fishy."

At this point, Hannah had to agree. Every issue that would have covered anything to do with the festival would have been in either the June or July boxes.

"I don't know what to say, Hannah. I'll check with my staff to see if anyone moved them for some reason, but if they don't know anything, I'll put in a call to my predecessor."

They climbed back up the stairs to the main newsroom. “Do I have to give back my scone and coffee?” Jack asked, trying to lighten the mood a bit.

She smiled at his effort. “They’re yours to enjoy. And I’ll still call Monroe. I’ll let you know what she says.”

“And I’ll let you know what I find out about the missing issues.”

Hannah headed back out to Main Street, undecided what to do with herself now that the time she’d allotted for research was no longer needed for that purpose.

She wandered toward the Blackberry Market and was drawn in by displays of fresh fruit. Cooking always helped clear her mind, so maybe she should pick up some produce and create a dessert to take to Lacy’s for the puzzle group tonight.

After chatting with owner Joe Wilson and making her selections, Hannah’s spirits were a little lighter. Since it was now what she would call a decent hour, she looped the shopping bag over her arm and called Monroe’s number.

The call went straight to voicemail, but a few moments later, Hannah’s phone signaled a text message.

I’m in rehearsal out at the festival grounds. Unless it’s an emergency, I’ll call you when we’re done.

No emergency, Hannah texted back. See you at Puzzle Night?

Monroe sent back a thumbs-up emoji.

Hannah realized that with Monroe tied up at the festival grounds, this might be a perfect opportunity to talk to Beverly Conley.

Deciding that she would soften her unexpected arrival, Hannah detoured to Sweet Caroline’s Bakery to pick up some morning buns.

As she recalled, Beverly had a sweet tooth. She made sure to leave room for dessert whenever she visited the Hot Spot.

After dropping her berries at home, Hannah grabbed her treats and notebook and hopped in her trusty Subaru. It would be more polite to call ahead, but if she wanted the truth, it might be better not to give advance warning or a chance to decline the visit. One thing Hannah knew for sure, Beverly was too much the consummate Southern hostess to turn a visitor away at the door.

Hannah had to rethink that assumption a short time later as she stood on the porch and rang the bell to no avail. She was about to give up when she saw a curtain twitch. Suspicious now, Hannah knocked on the doorframe and called through the screen. "Hello, Beverly? It's Hannah. I brought some morning buns and hoped we could visit a bit."

There was still no answer, so Hannah was about to give up when she saw Beverly slowly approaching the screen door.

"Good morning, Hannah. I'm sorry I didn't answer right away. I've been feeling a bit poorly and not really up to visitors. Monroe isn't here."

"I'm sorry you're unwell. I guess all the excitement can be a little too much."

Beverly gave a faint nod. Something was definitely worrying her.

"I was hoping I could speak to you about something," Hannah said.

After a long silence, Beverly relented and opened the door. "Come in, Hannah." She led Hannah down the hallway to the kitchen. "Would you like some coffee? I was about to make some."

Hannah nodded. "That would be lovely and will go well with the morning buns I brought from Sweet Caroline's."

That suggestion, at last, drew a slight smile. Beverly started the coffee, then went to the cupboard and took down some cups and saucers, dessert plates, and a platter. Hannah transferred the buns from the bakery box to the platter. In minutes, both women were seated at the table, each with a cup of coffee and a bun.

Beverly reached for her coffee cup with a hand that shook.

Hannah caught it and held it gently between her own. "I knew Monroe wouldn't be here," she confessed. "I was hoping to speak with you privately."

Beverly's face turned ashen. "Did you discover something?"

"No," Hannah assured her. "But Monroe is very concerned about how upset you are. I thought maybe you might confide in me about why."

Beverly slid her hands to her lap, but Hannah could tell from the taut muscles in her forearms that she was clenching them into fists.

"I'm sure I have nothing to confide, Hannah," she murmured. "I don't know what gave you the idea I did."

"You mentioned that you were a suspect in the original theft."

"I was, but I was exonerated. It was all a misunderstanding."

Something about her tone belied Beverly's words, so Hannah pressed on. "I've been wondering about it though. You're Eddie's wife. Why would they suspect you in the first place?"

"As I said, it was a misunderstanding. Someone told the police that Eddie and I had been arguing about how much time he spent on the road. It was no secret that I wanted him to stay home more."

"Which he did after the mandolin disappeared."

"Yes, but his rift with Ward nearly destroyed him. As much as I wanted him home with me, I would never have intentionally caused him harm."

Hannah believed Beverly was telling the truth about that. But something still didn't sit right. Beverly was far too nervous for someone who had simply been misunderstood. "You said you had an alibi?"

Beverly fiddled with her napkin. The morning bun sat untouched on her plate. "Yes. I was visiting with a—a friend."

Hannah could tell there was more to the story, but it was clear as day that Beverly had no intention of sharing her secrets. Hannah sipped her coffee. Finally, she set the cup aside. "Beverly, I'm not here to cause you distress, and I can see that I am. So I'll leave. But please know that I care about you, and I want to do whatever I can to help. Monroe was a dear friend when we were young, and you were like another grandmother to me. I would never do anything to hurt you, but Monroe asked me to help so she could ease your mind. If there comes a time you want to tell me something, you know where to find me."

Beverly broke off a piece of the pastry and lifted it to her mouth, but before she could take a bite, she set it back down. She rested both hands on the table and took a deep breath before looking up to hold Hannah's gaze. "I have one request. For the sake of my husband, will you come to me with anything you find before you share it with anyone else?"

Hannah swallowed hard. That was as clear an admission of there being some secret as if Beverly had come right out and said so herself. What was she hiding?

"Hannah?"

The older woman's voice was strained, and Hannah's heart ached for the toll this was taking on her. But Sheriff Steele was investigating a felony. Hannah couldn't withhold evidence if she uncovered it. "If I find any clues about what happened to the mandolin or the money, I have to report it to the sheriff first."

Beverly waved off Hannah's words. "I understand. I'm speaking of anything of a more personal nature. Anything that could hurt Eddie."

Hannah didn't want to agree to the request, but Beverly was leaving her little choice. "I will if I can," she said at last. Wondering all the while what Beverly might be hiding from her husband.

Chapter Ten

Hannah was still mulling over Beverly's odd request hours later when she arrived at Lacy's for Puzzle Night. She'd purposely arrived early to catch up with her friend, and because she was sure Lacy could use some help setting up, though she'd never admit it.

Hannah had parked around back, so she went to the kitchen door. "Knock, knock! I come bearing dessert."

"Hi, Hannah. Come on in."

Lacy's voice sounded weary—understandable as she was such a short time away from giving birth to her first child. Hannah found her sitting in the kitchen with her feet up on a stool. Lacy's hands rested on her stomach, and something stirred in Hannah's heart. God willing, she and Liam would someday be blessed with children. She was looking forward to sharing the joys of motherhood with her best friend.

"Come quick," Lacy said. "The baby is kicking. See it?"

Hannah gasped. She could indeed see the outline of a tiny foot pressing against Lacy's dress. "That's amazing. Oh, Lacy, I can't wait to meet this baby."

"You and me both," Lacy said with a grin. She shifted to a more comfortable position. "Now, why don't you tell me what's on your mind, and don't you even try to hide it from me. I know when something is up with you, and I don't need to be protected from anything. I have enough of that with Neil."

Hannah laughed. "That's sweet. He's going to be such a doting father."

"I imagine he'll have the baby's first book waiting with him in the birthing room. But enough evasion. What's bothering you? Is it the wedding planning? I can see the tension coming off you like smoke."

"How flattering." At Lacy's raised eyebrows, Hannah gave in. "It's not wedding planning, though we should talk about that. It's Monroe and Beverly. Beverly mostly. She's a wreck about something related to this mandolin, but she won't say what it is."

"You don't think she's the one who stole it, do you?"

"No, I don't." Hannah was confident about that. "I really don't believe she took it and certainly not that she broke it, but she is definitely hiding something."

Hannah went on to fill Lacy in on the initial visit to the Conleys' house with Colin, Monroe's panicked phone call, and finally her confusing meeting with Beverly earlier today.

"So she specifically asked you to share any personal evidence you found with her before going to law enforcement? That is odd."

"I was hoping you might have some thoughts on what she could be hiding, because I have no idea."

"She said she was a suspect because she wanted Eddie to stop touring?"

"Yes."

"But you don't think she would have gone to extremes to stop him."

"No, I saw her face when Monroe showed him the mandolin. She was shedding tears of joy. According to Monroe, the change came after Eddie said he was investigating, but I think it happened after Colin interviewed her."

"Did you ask him about it?"

Hannah smacked her forehead. "I haven't seen him since Saturday. I don't know if he can actually tell me what she said, but I should ask, right?"

Lacy laughed. "I actually meant Eddie, but I do think it makes sense to ask Colin too. If he can't reveal what Beverly said, at least you'll alert him to her state of mind."

"You're right. And I will talk to Eddie. Monroe said he spends most days fishing on his dock. I'll find a time to go visit him."

"I know Beverly has a regular appointment at the hairdresser's on Tuesday mornings, so you could probably squeeze it in before the Hot Spot opens."

"That's good to know. I'll keep you posted." The sound of cars outside was quickly followed by happy, chattering voices, so Lacy and Hannah tabled the conversation.

Soon Lacy's kitchen was filled with the sounds of friends happy to be together. Connie Sanchez, the Grace Community Church secretary, surprised Lacy with a present—two nursery rhyme puzzles. "I thought we could assemble them tonight and then I'll glue and frame them for you to hang in the nursery. So when you're alone with your little one, you'll still feel the love of your friends with you."

Lacy's eyes welled with happy tears. "You all are the best friends a woman could ask for. This baby is lucky to have so many honorary aunts."

As the friends laughed and chatted while they completed the adorable puzzles, Hannah was glad to see Beverly fitting right in, but she was also confused. Beverly had either set her worries aside for the evening or was doing a good job of hiding them, because she seemed to be actually enjoying herself. There was no hint of the troubled woman Hannah had spoken with earlier and no mention of Eddie or the mandolin mystery. The only explanation Hannah could think of was that Beverly didn't want to reveal any of her worries to her friends.

Hannah was also impressed, though not surprised, by those friends' sensitivity. The return of the mandolin was the hottest topic in Blackberry Valley, but no one tried to question either Monroe or Beverly about it.

However, once Monroe and her grandmother headed out early—Monroe announced that she had a morning rehearsal, and her grandmother needed her rest—the restraint evaporated.

Hannah was suddenly deluged with questions. She didn't really have anything to share, but she was glad of the opportunity to tap into the memories of women who had been alive during the original festivals. "Does the name Maureen Hughes ring a bell for any of you?"

The women glanced at one another, but no sign of recognition dawned on anyone's face.

"Who is she, Hannah? Maybe the name would mean something in context," said Miriam Spencer, who was also in the church women's group with Hannah.

"Maureen was a newspaper reporter who published a number of articles about the final festival in the *Chronicle* back in the day. I went to the paper this morning and the boxes that contain those issues are all missing," Hannah said. "It made me a little suspicious.

I assume, as a reporter, she would have had full access to the festival grounds, including the backstage area."

"Did you say Hughes?" Connie had been rinsing glasses at the sink, but now she wiped her hands on a dish towel and approached the table.

"I did," Hannah confirmed. "Maureen Hughes. Did you know her?"

"More like I knew *of* her. She made a big name for herself when her reports about the festival caught some big-city editor's eye. Some say she bought her way out of the holler with those stories." *Holler* was the word *hollow* with an exaggerated Southern accent.

Hannah was hooked. "Why would they say that?"

Miriam laughed. "I remember her now. For starters, she wrote a book called *Out of the Holler.* It was a memoir that angered quite a few people, though I hear it was a bestseller."

Evangeline picked up the story. "I read it when it came out. I always felt like she was trying to capitalize on Loretta Lynn's success with *Coal Miner's Daughter.* The tone was totally different though. Loretta's book honored her family, and you could feel her love and respect. Maureen's was rather disparaging of the place and family she came from. She focused a lot on the feuding, the poverty, and how lucky she had been to escape it."

"That's unpleasant, but what could it have to do with the missing mandolin?" Hannah asked.

"Maybe nothing, but Maureen was part of the Hughes clan. It's coming back to me," Evangeline said. "I remember there being a lot of speculation at the beginning of the festival that summer about why someone from a feuding family was in Blackberry Valley to cover the enemy's festival."

"Whoa, back up," Hannah said. "What feud? The only feud I know of is the one between Ward Burton and Eddie Conley after Eddie accused Ward of stealing his mandolin."

Miriam laughed. "Oh, Hannah. You know feuding is as much a part of these mountains as the music is. Just think about that mystery you solved with the Haleys and the Bentons. They feuded for years, all because a puppy got loose and two friends didn't trust each other. Imagine how a grudge could be held over a stolen mandolin."

"True," Hannah said begrudgingly. As much as she hated it, friendships did often end over simple misunderstandings.

"I'm just saying that when there's bad blood, nothing is off-limits," Miriam said. "There was plenty of bad blood between Ward Burton's family and the Hugheses, going back a couple of generations. Their feud started with a runaway bride, but the details were forgotten and only the hatred lived on. It didn't help bring peace when Ward and Eddie made a name for themselves with their festival."

Evangeline weighed in again. "Everyone talks about how wonderful the festival years were, but no one talks about the raid the second year or the fires that broke out and nearly ruined the festival another year."

"All of this is news to me," Hannah admitted.

"I was just a little kid at the time of the raid, so I don't remember all the details," Evangeline said. "I do remember being terrified when these masked people came racing through the field during one of the concerts. I didn't want to go back the next year, but my mother told me it had just been the Hughes brothers dressed up, and we had nothing to worry about."

"I remember that," Miriam added. "I was there with my husband. It was scary even for me."

"What about the fires?"

"Those were even more dangerous," Miriam responded. "I'm thinking that was in 1972. At least one night of the festival was canceled when a series of fires broke out on the edge of the campground right before the opening act."

"I remember hearing that several teens from the Hughes clan were arrested for that," Connie said. "But that seemed to end the trouble. The last few years were great until the mandolin disappeared."

Hannah's thoughts immediately turned to the fire Liam had been called to the night before they'd found the mandolin. She hoped no one was reigniting the feud. She wondered why Patrick hadn't mentioned those other fires, and made a mental note to give him a call.

Miriam chimed back in. "The feuding really heated up one other summer. I think it was back in '69. Romance again. One of the Burton girls got hitched with one of the Hughes boys. They shared a love of music, and rumor had it they'd be performing at the festival. Someone in the family was determined to stop it." She gave a rueful smile. "I have to admit, at the time, I found it all rather romantic."

"Are you saying that Maureen Hughes may have come here to cause trouble because of the feud? That she could have stolen the mandolin as part of it? And then she wrote newspaper articles about it?" Hannah asked. "That doesn't really make sense, because the mandolin belonged to Eddie, not Ward."

"Stealing Eddie's mandolin did end the festival, though," Miriam countered. "So if ruining it was the thief's intent, it worked.

I'm not saying anything for sure, but I imagine the sheriff at the time would have questioned her, given the family history."

All the more reason Hannah needed to see what was in the case records. Was it only this morning that she'd bemoaned the lack of clues? She should be careful what she wished for. She'd gone from having no clues to a plethora of possible ones—but still no concrete evidence.

When Hannah headed out the next morning, she hoped that Eddie could help her make sense of everything that was spinning in her brain, but she also wanted to hear what changed his mind about seeking out who had broken his mandolin. What happened in his meeting with Sheriff Steele to make him decide to investigate on his own?

Last night, Monroe had mentioned that she would drop her grandmother off at the hair salon on her way to her own rehearsal, so Hannah waited until nine to be sure there was no chance of passing them on their way into town. She retraced the route she'd traveled with Colin and then steered her Subaru up the Conleys' long driveway. She left the car, then strolled around the house and across the lawn toward the lake. As she reached the crest of the hill, she could see that, as expected, Eddie sat on the dock with his fishing pole extended over the pond. Slowly, she made her way down the hill, not wanting to alarm him.

"Don't scare my fish away, Hannah Prentiss."

So much for Eddie being alarmed. "You don't seem surprised that I'm here."

"I knew it was a matter of time, and since the ladies of the house are out..." He shrugged as if the rest were obvious.

"Did Monroe talk to you?"

"About asking you to solve the mystery? No. But I overheard her reassuring Bev."

Hannah came around and lowered herself to sit cross-legged on the dock in front of him. "May I ask you a question?"

He chuckled. "Isn't that what you came out here for?"

"Why did you decide to investigate on your own?"

Eddie didn't answer at first, but Hannah sat patiently while he baited his hook and flicked the line out over the lake. "If you were in my shoes, would you wait for answers?"

Hannah mulled the question over. She obviously knew the answer. She was involved now, and it wasn't even her life that had been turned on its end. But how could she answer Eddie in a way that would encourage him to back off and allow his wife to relax?

"I guess that would depend. It's no secret that I have a thing for investigating mysteries. But I think if I knew it would deeply upset someone I loved, I'd have to give it up."

"Then you're a stronger person than I am."

It was ingrained in Hannah to be respectful of her elders, but if she didn't push Eddie, she couldn't solve the mystery. She'd simply have to try to be polite with her questions. "Why can't you give it up for Beverly?" she asked gently. "No one is asking you to live without answers. Just to let the sheriff investigate."

Eddie pushed his fishing cap back on his head, and Hannah could clearly see the frown etched in his face. "Whoever broke my mandolin, broke me," he replied, his voice soft, but shaky with emotion. "At least, that's what I've told myself all these years. How does a man forget that?" He gazed out over the water for a long minute. "I tried playing again, but I never found anyone I meshed with the way I did with Ward, so I stuck to playing for my family—and the fish," he finished with a sad grin.

Hannah switched direction. "Do you know why your plan to investigate has your wife so worked up?"

Her question was again met with silence as Eddie's fishing line went taut. Eddie reeled it in, looked the fish over, and deftly released it. "I reckon it has something to do with her being a suspect," he finally said. "They ruled her out, you know, but she was mortified all the same. Didn't show her face in town for a long while after that."

Hannah nodded, but there was an undercurrent to his statement that disturbed her. He knew his wife's shame, but he was still bent on investigating. To prove her innocence beyond all doubt by identifying the real culprit? Or was there some other reason? She had a feeling that, like his wife, he wasn't sharing everything. What secrets was Eddie keeping? Despite his words, he was really no more forthcoming than Beverly had been. Hannah decided it was time to take a more direct approach. "Is there someone you suspect?"

"I thought you were the one doing the investigating."

"I am, but I wasn't even born when all this went down, so if you know something, it would be helpful if you shared."

"The sheriff's department investigated. They found no evidence of anyone taking it. Of course there weren't surveillance cameras back then like there are now."

Eddie's voice had a resigned quality, but Hannah kept pushing. "Was there anyone who would have had a reason to steal your mandolin?"

"Now we're getting somewhere." Eddie rebaited his hook and sent the line flying again.

For a second, Hannah wondered if he was playing with her the same way he played with the fish. She decided to wait him out.

"According to the sheriff, there were as many suspects as there are fish in this lake."

This was surprising news to Hannah, and it made little sense. She shifted uncomfortably on the dock. The sun beat down on her face, and she wished she'd thought to wear a sun hat. She shaded her eyes with her hand and gazed out over the lake. "That's a lot of suspects."

He merely grunted.

"Why?" Hannah pressed. "I find it hard to believe you had so many enemies."

Eddie huffed out a breath. "It wasn't enemies Sheriff Crane was thinking of, though I guess I had my fair share of those. He was talking about all the fans at the festival. After mounting a sham investigation, he wrote off the theft as an overzealous fan wanting a souvenir." His voice was raw with resentment.

Hannah couldn't completely understand his attachment to the mandolin, but it wasn't a stretch to believe that the sheriff dismissing Eddie's loss had upset him. Hannah had once believed that she'd lost a ring her mother had given her, and she'd been distraught until she'd found it again.

She also now understood his unwillingness to believe that Colin would solve the case.

"How did he explain the missing money? Was that allegedly stolen by a fan too?"

Eddie smiled. "According to Sheriff Crane, the money wasn't stolen. It burned up in the ticket booth fire."

Hannah was growing stiff, so she straightened her legs and leaned back with her hands planted on the deck behind her. "The fire department report said otherwise."

Eddie's gaze narrowed. "And how do you know that?"

Hannah grinned. "I have an in with the former fire chief." She waved her left hand, and the round diamond in its white filigree setting flashed in the sunlight. "I'm engaged to his grandson, the current fire chief."

Eddie gave a snort of laughter. "Go on. I'm listening."

She relayed her conversation with Patrick, repeating what he'd told her about the timing, the ash, and the impossibility that all the proceeds had burned.

Eddie's fishing pole lay limp in his hands as he pondered Hannah's words. She could almost see his mind processing the news.

He had taken her bait, so now Hannah reeled him in. "Back to my original question. Setting aside your angry blaming of Ward, who do you really think stole the mandolin? Was it someone from the Hughes family settling an old score?"

Eddie sized her up. "I'm beginning to understand why Monroe asked for your help. I'll make you a deal, Hannah Prentiss. I'll tell you what I think, but you need to keep it between us until you have proof."

"Between us and the sheriff, and only if you promise to abandon your investigation and leave it to Sheriff Steele and me. I guarantee he won't brush this off the way Sheriff Crane did."

Eddie held out his hand to shake hers. "You've got yourself a deal."

Chapter Eleven

Hannah was in her Subaru on her way back from Eddie's home when her phone rang. She answered on her hands-free system. "Hi, Colin. Are you calling to tell me you solved the mystery?"

She could hear his laughter. "I was calling to see if you already had."

"No such luck, but I did just have an interesting conversation with Eddie Conley. He gave me his short list of suspects."

Colin made a disgruntled sound. "He wasn't so forthcoming with me."

"I don't think his reticence had anything to do with you, and everything to do with one of your predecessors." She relayed Eddie's version of how the case had basically been dismissed as having to do with a fan's greed.

The sheriff gave a heavy sigh. "That tracks with what I've found in the case files. I was actually calling to say you're free to come look them over anytime that's convenient, but I have to warn you that there's not much here."

"How about now? I'll fill you in on Eddie's list and take a look at what you have. I can be there in about fifteen minutes."

"Works for me."

When Hannah arrived at the police station, receptionist Vanessa Lodge was busy on a phone call. But she waved Hannah back and mouthed, "He's expecting you."

Hannah walked down the corridor and knocked on the sheriff's open door.

Colin glanced up from the pile of papers he was studying. "Hi, Hannah. Come on in. I was going to set us up in the conference room, but there's not enough here to warrant it."

She was shocked. "How can a felony investigation have such a small paper trail?"

"Funny you should mention that. Sheriff Crane did not consider it a felony investigation."

Hannah blinked. "Come again? I thought you said that the theft of the mandolin was a felony on its own."

"I did. However, Sheriff Crane treated them as two separate cases. He wrote off the missing cash as accidental loss due to the fire. The mandolin investigation went nowhere and was quickly closed for lack of evidence."

"I'm confused." Hannah massaged her temples. "Isn't the police report reliant on the fire department report?"

"The departments should work together. Liam and I do. If he tells me something is arson, I'm going to trust his expertise and treat it as a crime."

"But Patrick Berthold told me that the fire department report classified the fire at the ticket booth as arson. He also stated that there was insufficient evidence to claim that all the money burned."

"Well, that puts an interesting twist on it. There is absolutely no mention of that report in the case files."

Hannah was thoughtful. "Does that make Sheriff Crane a suspect?"

Colin shook his head wearily. "Maybe, or maybe just inept."

"Is there any indication he was open to bribes?"

The sheriff's expression sharpened. "That's a serious allegation, and I would not want to make it without proof. I can't rule it out, but department gossip leans more toward characterizing Crane as lazy than corrupt." He gestured toward the scant pile of evidence. "I'd say this case file bears that out."

"May I look at it?"

"Do you want to tell me what Mr. Conley had to say first?"

"Sure," Hannah replied. "That way we can discuss whether there's anything in the file that gives merit to his suspicions." She reached into her handbag and withdrew her pen and notebook.

"Highly doubtful, but I like your optimism."

"To start, let me be clear that Eddie was not accusing anyone. He was frustrated and honestly offended by how Sheriff Crane dismissed the theft. Eddie felt that there were at least a few people who had motive, though he was clear he had no evidence to point to any of them."

"Understood." The sheriff took out his own notebook and pen. "Who's first on the list?"

"Eddie's manager, Martin Lowe."

Colin's eyebrows shot up. "Bad blood with his management?"

"Not exactly. Eddie said that he and Ward Burton were on the verge of splitting up anyway. The stolen mandolin just accelerated the timeline. As Monroe told us, they'd been arguing about the future of the Blackberry Mountain Boys, whether to amplify their sound or not."

"Right. Ward wanted to expand into bigger venues."

"Yes, and Eddie cared more about connecting personally with the fans and creating a bond with the music. I think that added to the insult of Sheriff Crane suggesting a fan had stolen the instrument. It went against his idea of his relationship with his fans."

"Understandable. But let's get back to your main point. Many artists manage to create a bond even in huge arenas. Why couldn't Eddie have done that?"

Hannah waved off the argument. "Maybe he could have, but it's irrelevant because it was Eddie's stubborn belief about it that was causing the rift. Anyway, Martin Lowe stood to lose his income from managing them if the band broke up."

"But for argument's sake, many bands break up, and the headliners continue in solo careers or form a new band. Bluegrass history is rife with that kind of story."

Hannah's eyes widened. "I didn't know you were such a bluegrass buff."

The sheriff grinned. "I did some reading up on it last night, and Genevieve knew a lot. She has some family members who play."

"Your wife has an intriguing background."

Colin's eyes lit up as they always did when talking about his wife. "That she does. My point was that the band breaking up didn't necessarily mean their manager would be out of money. Didn't he go on to manage Ward Burton's new band?"

"He did. Anyway, I'm not saying he should be a suspect, just that Eddie considered him one. And if he did go on to manage Ward's new band, that could explain why Eddie blamed him. He would have been able to guess that Eddie's mandolin going missing would have brought on the breakup sooner. And then he could work with Ward, whose big ideas were where the big money was."

"Not a bad theory," Colin said, making notes.

Hannah glanced down at the notepad where she'd jotted all Eddie's suspects once she'd gotten back in her car after their visit. "His second suspect falls into basically the same category, of wanting to make more money from bigger venues. Arthur White was the festival promoter."

"His grandson is behind the new festival, isn't he?"

"Yes," Hannah replied. "Do you think you should talk to him?"

"Wouldn't hurt, though I assume he wouldn't have been alive back then. Still, he might have heard something. Did Eddie have anyone else in mind?"

Hannah settled back in her chair. "Everyone from the concession stand operator to the cranky neighbor who kept trying to get the festival shut down. We talked about him the other day." At the sheriff's nod, Hannah continued. "I brought up another name. Maureen Hughes."

"Who is that?"

"She was a journalist. Wrote a couple of articles for the *Chronicle* about the festival."

Colin frowned. "Why would you suspect her?"

"Because her family had been feuding with Ward Burton's family for generations."

The sheriff looked intrigued. "Tell me more."

Hannah recapped what she had learned from the women at Puzzle Night. "I brought up Maureen's name to Eddie. He dismissed her as a suspect because her family's feud was with Ward, not him, but I'm not so sure that mattered. If Ward's success as part of the Blackberry Mountain Boys was salt in the wound, then it makes sense that they'd want to destroy the band, no matter who got hurt in the process. As a member of the press, Maureen would have had access to all areas of the festival, from backstage to the area around the ticket booth."

"Makes sense," Colin murmured.

Hannah set her notepad aside and leaned forward. "That's not all. I couldn't read her articles online, so I went to the *Chronicle*. Jack Delaney took me down to the basement archives. The bins containing all the issues related to the festival were missing."

Colin rested his elbows on his desk and steepled his hands. "Okay, that sounds suspicious on the surface, but when did they go missing? And what purpose would it serve to hide issues of a newspaper with articles that had already been read by most of the people in town? Presumably she didn't write anything that would implicate herself in the theft of the mandolin, or even the incompetent Sheriff Crane would have had to arrest her."

Hannah sat back, deflated. "True. Still, I would like to try to find her and talk to her. Maybe she saw something that she didn't write about. Or maybe she did take the mandolin and made sure to throw suspicion in another direction."

"Not impossible, but let's not put all our eggs in that basket. What about the storage company? Eddie didn't mention them?"

"No." Hannah twirled her pen between her fingers. "They certainly need to be investigated, but Eddie never brought them up, and I don't like them as the thieves."

"Because?"

"Well, for starters, they weren't even involved until almost a decade later, when Beverly hired them to pack up the shack and put everything in storage. Sure, one of them could have stolen the cash if it was hidden in the storage shack. To the best of my knowledge, which admittedly is not much, none of them had anything to do with the festival. So, money aside, the most they could be guilty of is damaging the mandolin after it was already left in storage."

"That makes sense."

"Does the case file say anything much about Beverly Conley as a suspect?"

Colin sorted through the pile of papers and handed one to Hannah.

She quickly perused the paper, noting some coffee stains. Clearly, the former sheriff had made little effort to be careful with evidence. When she'd finished reading, she leaned back in her chair. "This matches what Beverly and Eddie both told me. She was an initial suspect because a number of people reported that she and Eddie had been fighting about how much time he spent on the road. She wanted him home more. They had a young child, and she didn't like being left alone."

"But she was cleared quickly."

"Yes, Eddie said he defended her. Sure they fought, but they loved each other, and she would never do something so vindictive."

"You know her. Do you agree?"

"I do. She told me the same thing, and every memory I have of them is as a genuinely loving couple. She also had an alibi, as is noted in the file."

Colin rested his elbows on his desk and leaned his forehead into his hands. "This all leads us to suspects who are either dead or alibied. Unless we stumble on some long-hidden evidence, there's nothing in here to point us in the right direction." He waved his hand over the case file. "Eddie Conley deserves better than to have another sheriff dismiss his concerns, so I'll do what I can to dig deeper."

Hannah gave him a sheepish look. "Thank you. I kind of gave Eddie a guarantee that both of us would take the case seriously and pursue any leads we can find."

Colin's phone rang. "I have to take this." He picked up the receiver, listened, thanked the caller, and hung up. "That was Vanessa reminding me I have a meeting. I can set you up in the conference room if you want to read through this file."

"Thanks. I know you said it isn't much, but I'd like to at least see what was done. Just for context."

"Sure. Come with me." Colin gathered up the papers and led Hannah down the hall to a small room. "Just let Vanessa know when you're done, and she'll secure the file. Stay in touch, okay?"

"Of course."

Once she was alone, Hannah checked her phone to make sure there were no messages from anyone at the Hot Spot. She still had some time to spare before she needed to head in, so she got right to work.

Colin had not been kidding when he said there was little here. There was an initial police report from the scene and a few faded photographs that had apparently not been protected against deterioration. They were just tossed into the folder. The ink on the reports was faded and difficult to read, so Hannah grabbed her phone and opened a magnifying app. She was better able to read the words, but soon realized there was nothing in that report that she didn't already know.

There was another paper with some barely legible comments that looked like notes from witness interviews. The only names familiar to Hannah were the members of the Blackberry Mountain Boys and their family members. There was a witness statement from Eddie and an alibi statement from Beverly, but nothing to indicate that her alibi had been checked. That was interesting.

Both papers were stained with what looked like rings from a coffee cup. Hannah shook her head. Inept or incompetent seemed like kind words to describe Sheriff Crane. Little wonder neither the mandolin nor the money had ever been located.

She would have to see what she and Colin could do to rectify that.

Chapter Twelve

Hannah left the police station feeling frustrated, to put it mildly. If the former sheriff hadn't properly done his job back then, how was she supposed to solve the mystery fifty years later? But Monroe and Eddie were counting on her.

The responsibility weighed heavily on Hannah's shoulders, but for now she had to set it aside and focus on her restaurant. En route to the Hot Spot to prep for the evening, she called Monroe. She wanted to let her know that Eddie had agreed to halt his investigation and leave it up to Hannah and Sheriff Steele. She also had to ask about the interview with Jack, which she'd forgotten to do at Puzzle Night. Monroe didn't pick up, so Hannah left a voicemail and then headed to the kitchen.

After racing around all morning, she was starving, so she dug inside the industrial fridge in search of leftovers. Jacob had created an amazing summer vegetable quiche on Saturday night, and Hannah was thrilled to find a hefty slice wrapped in plastic.

She heated it up enough to take the chill off, then grabbed a glass of tea and settled in a corner booth with her lunch and a notebook. None of her staff had arrived yet, so she could focus on the mystery while she ate. It was time to make a plan of action for her investigation.

First on the list was to call Liam's granddad and ask if he had any information about the fires during the other years of the festival. If there had been a pattern, that might yield clues.

She also needed to do some digging to locate Maureen Hughes. Hopefully the journalist had an author website with some contact information, though if she had been working in the seventies, Maureen may be long retired by now.

Then there was the storage company. Hannah made a note to check with Monroe about her rehearsal schedule to see if there was a morning she might be free to accompany Hannah to speak with them. It seemed prudent to have a family member present if she expected the company to release information.

"Hi, Hannah. You look preoccupied. Thinking up new menu ideas, or doing accounts?"

Hannah swallowed her last bite and shook her head at Elaine. "Neither. Working on the mandolin mystery. I was out interviewing Eddie and then talking to Colin, so I was just updating my notes." She gathered her notebook and dirty dishes. "How are reservations looking for tonight?"

"Typical Tuesday so far, but I was just about to listen to the phone messages to see if there were any new requests."

"Let me just put these dishes in the kitchen, then I'll be out to help set up."

Raquel and Dylan arrived as Hannah entered the kitchen, and Jacob was tying the strings of his apron. She greeted everyone and then held up the empty plate. "The veggie quiche was superb, Jacob. I hope you're putting it on tonight's menu too."

"Oh, yes," Raquel gushed. "Everyone raved about it. Light, which makes it perfect for a summer evening, but filling too."

"How can I not then?" Jacob made a face. "I was going to debut a bluegrass barbecue special, but—"

"Can we do both if I chop the veggies for the quiche?" Hannah offered. The other two laughed at Jacob's feigned gasp of horror. Hannah put her hands on her hips. "I vow to keep my head in the game and make them look like real vegetables. I have to go check with Elaine about tonight's reservations, but then I'll be back to get chopping."

"No need." Elaine pushed through the swinging doors. "I was coming to ask how you feel about another party from the festival. It will be larger this time because the musicians have begun to arrive."

"Oh, right. Monroe has been in rehearsals." Hannah turned to her team. "What do you say? Can we do this?"

Raquel and Dylan exchanged glances. "We can," they chimed.

"Jacob? I know the burden falls mainly on you, but I'll do whatever you need, and I promise to stay focused on the food."

"Sure. The more the merrier. It's not every restaurant that gets a bluegrass crowd. Maybe Marshall will put out more of a good word on the blog."

"I'll call and drop a hint," Raquel said with a wink.

Hannah thanked her team. "You guys really are the best crew a restaurant owner could ask for."

Elaine waved a hand in dismissal as she left the kitchen. "I'll call back and confirm that they're welcome."

Raquel and Dylan headed for the dining room to start folding napkins and arranging place settings while Hannah and Jacob got to work on the food. The prep time flew, and soon they were running like a well-oiled machine to manage a busier-than-usual Tuesday.

Hours later, when Raquel ferried the final plate out to a patron, Hannah and Jacob high-fived before collapsing on stools. "That was stupendous," she said when she caught her breath.

"That's one word for it," Jacob replied. "I was thinking more like exhausting. But it was invigorating too, wasn't it?"

Hannah nodded. "It reminded me of my days as a chef in California. It's good to know I still have the chops." She turned and looked at the stacks of dirty dishes that still awaited them, then closed her eyes. "Let's take a break before we tackle the kitchen."

When Jacob didn't respond, she opened her eyes. He was no longer on the stool, but standing by the swinging door. He put a finger to his lips and waved her over.

Hannah came and looked over his shoulder to see into the dining room. Most of the diners had left. There were just a few tables with couples finishing their meals.

In the back section, where Elaine had grouped tables together for the festival crowd, the chairs had been pulled away from the tables and arranged in a circle. The musicians had exchanged knives and forks for their instruments and seemed to be holding an impromptu jam session. The unmistakable sounds of bluegrass music filled the Hot Spot dining room, and not from the sound system.

Hannah untied her apron and tossed it aside before slipping quietly through the doors, with Jacob right behind her. "I know this song," Hannah told him. "'Footprints in the Snow.'"

Jacob kept his voice low. "I didn't know you were a bluegrass fan."

"I went to see a band with my father and his cousin last year. The band performed this song. I liked it, so I looked it up afterward."

The musicians started on "Blue Moon of Kentucky."

"I grew up on the Elvis version of this, but there's something about the bluegrass that sounds better," Hannah murmured to her chef.

"It's that high, lonesome sound," Jacob told her, tapping his toes.

"You're so right."

"A chef has to understand the music and culture if he's going to get the recipes right."

Raquel joined them. "You sure got the recipe right for that barbecue special. Everyone loved it." She turned to Hannah. "I hope it was okay to let them do this. We checked with the other patrons, and they were thrilled at the chance to witness a preview of the festival."

"I love it." Hannah leaned back against the wall to enjoy the concert. Her goal in opening the Hot Spot had been to create a place where people came for the best farm-to-table dining, but she'd also wanted it to be a place where friends and strangers felt welcome. Over the past year, there had been many notable moments of success, and tonight felt like watching that dream come to life yet again.

When the last song wound down and the remaining diners rose to applaud the performance, Hannah stepped forward to greet the musicians. She introduced herself and thanked them for sharing their music.

A tall man in a suit leaned his upright bass against the table and rose to greet her. "Thank you for welcoming us, Ms. Prentiss. I'm Howard Burton, but everyone calls me Junior to avoid confusion with my father, Ward Burton. Thank you for letting us take over the Hot Spot tonight. Playing with friends is one of our favorite ways of winding down."

Hannah extended her hand to shake his, pleased to meet the son of Eddie's ex-partner. "My pleasure, Junior. Feel free to make the Hot Spot your home away from home while you're here. And that means calling me Hannah," she added with a smile. "This has been such a treat for us tonight. May I ask for an encore?"

Junior turned to his friends, who enthusiastically agreed. "Do you have any requests?" he asked Hannah.

"I do, if you don't mind. When I was a girl, my dad used to play a record of Bill Monroe performing a gospel medley. It started out with 'Swing Low, Sweet Chariot' and was always one of my favorites."

The guitar player strummed a few notes, and Hannah smiled. "Yes, that's it."

"Then it will be our pleasure. That medley is one of our favorite closing numbers. It's bluegrass with our gospel roots."

Just as the group picked up their instruments and settled back down, Hannah saw Liam in the doorway. She crossed over to stand with him and explained what was happening. Liam wrapped his arm around her as the music began, and Hannah leaned her head on his shoulder. She tapped her toes and mouthed the words as the song resonated through her body, her worries carried away on the music.

When the final notes faded, she brought Liam over to meet Junior, who then introduced the players. Hannah in turn introduced her team, who had served them all night. They'd already expressed their appreciation to Elaine, Raquel, and Dylan, but when she introduced Jacob, they gave him a round of applause.

"That barbecue was good enough to make the angels sing," the Dobro player enthused.

Jacob humbly accepted their praise and welcomed them back for his version of an encore the following night.

By the time everyone left and Hannah and her crew finished cleaning up, it was nearly midnight. Hannah and Liam were enjoying a late-night snack in the kitchen when his phone alerted. She simultaneously heard the fire truck sirens as they raced down the street.

"What's going on?" she asked Liam.

Her stomach twisted at his answer. "It's another fire out at the festival grounds."

Chapter Thirteen

Liam rose from his seat. "Colt and Archer headed out, but I should join them."

"I'd like to come," Hannah said. "There's something I learned that might have to do with these fires."

"That's fine. Just promise you'll stay out of danger." They hurried out to his Jeep Rubicon. Liam listened intently as Hannah relayed what she'd learned from her friends while they'd been assembling puzzles at Lacy's table. They zipped through the quiet night in the direction the fire truck had gone. He seemed surprised to hear about the other fires. "I wonder why Gramps didn't mention them."

"I was asking him specifically about the ticket booth fire in 1976. He wouldn't necessarily have had reason to connect that with fires in '72. Connie said that some teenagers from the Hughes family were arrested for starting those."

"If it weren't so late, I'd call him and ask, but that'll have to wait until morning. Has anything else come up in your investigation that makes these fires more suspicious than they seem on the surface?"

"That's hard to say without knowing more about what the fire department concluded back then. The only connection I've been able to hypothesize is between the feuding Hughes and Burton families."

"Any relation to Junior?"

"Probably. I assume he was too young to be involved in any feuding, but I should make time to talk with him, see what he heard."

"Maybe wait until we hear what Gramps says. We wouldn't want to ruin this year's festival by unnecessarily bringing up bad memories."

"He's a wise man, my fiancé," Hannah teased.

"Don't you go forgetting it," Liam shot right back with laughter in his voice as he pulled up behind the fire truck. "I know you won't stay in the Jeep, but remember you promised to stay out of danger."

"I will. I honestly want to wander around the campgrounds and get a feel for the place. Dad told me this is the same field they used for the original festivals. I thought it might help me visualize the setting better to see it myself."

Liam headed over to where Colt and Archer already had things under control, but Hannah struck out in the opposite direction. The spotlights from the fire truck illuminated the field, making it almost as bright as day. She could see the festival stage under construction on the far side of the field. Fortunately, the fire appeared to pose no threat to it, given the distance between them.

She was curious to know what Liam would determine about the cause of this fire. They knew of no intent to interrupt festival preparations, but two fires in under a week was unusual. She'd ask Liam about that too. Could they be the work of reckless pranksters, or was there something more sinister at play here?

Hannah's phone dinged with a message from Liam calling her back to the Jeep. She hurried across the field to where he waited for her.

"The fire was easily extinguished, but Colt and Archer are going to hang around a bit longer just to make sure no sparks have spread. There's no need for us to wait," he told her.

Hannah was relieved. She'd had a long, busy day and was eager to be in bed. As they drove back, she asked Liam her questions, and they tossed some ideas back and forth.

"There's nothing suspicious at this point, but I plan to keep a close eye on the festival grounds," he said. "I'll call Colin in the morning and talk to him about increasing security. With the festival so close now, I'd hate to see pranksters ruin it. If it is something more serious—well, we'll deal with it."

At the Hot Spot, Liam walked Hannah to the door of her apartment and kissed her good night. She was practically asleep on her feet by that time, so she carried the sweetness of his kiss with her to bed, hoping it would give her beautiful dreams.

Hannah felt like her head had barely hit the pillow when her phone rang the next morning. She groped around but only succeeded in knocking it off her bedside table. By the time she got herself up and found where the phone had slid under the bed, the ringing had stopped. She fished it out and saw the missed call was from Monroe, so rather than go back to sleep, she immediately called back.

"Hi, Hannah." The words sounded so perky that Hannah envisioned them surrounded by smiling emojis. How did Monroe sound so cheerful this early on a Wednesday morning?

Hannah pushed back her hair and fought through her grogginess, trying to sound happy about being awakened at the crack of dawn. "Good morning, Monroe."

"Oh, goodness. I'm sorry if I woke you. I was having breakfast with Nana and realized I never responded to your question about the storage company. Any chance you can go this morning? My mother is arriving this afternoon, so I'll be pretty tied up in sound checks and rehearsals for the rest of the week. It's been a while since we've performed together."

Rubbing the sleep from her eyes, Hannah replied, "Sure, we can do that. Do you want to drive?"

Monroe laughed. "That tired, huh? I heard you had an exciting jam session at the Hot Spot last night."

Hannah smiled at the memory. "It was awesome. They promised to come back. I hope you'll join them."

"Maybe."

Monroe's voice had lost some of its pep. What was that about? She'd have to ask on the way to the warehouse.

"How soon can you be ready?"

Hannah stifled a yawn before answering. "Twenty minutes? I need time for a quick shower and to make coffee if my questions are going to make any sense."

"You take the shower. I'll pick up some coffee from Zane. I assume he knows your order."

"He does. Thanks, Monroe. See you in twenty."

She hopped in the shower, dressed quickly, and was waiting downstairs when Monroe pulled up in her red convertible. "Fancy wheels you've got there."

"I bought it with my first contract. I'd always dreamed of driving a convertible. Buying this was a vote of confidence in myself and my career."

"Well-deserved, I'd say."

Monroe's face lost a bit of its glow. "Maybe."

That was the second question Monroe had answered with a vague response. Before Hannah could press her about it, Monroe changed the topic. "Nana gave me a copy of the receipt from the storage company, so we have the proof and authority to ask about it."

"Good." Hannah took a sip of the coffee Monroe brought for her and felt life begin to flow back into her veins. "I think we should phrase the questions as merely gathering background information from the company to help us figure it out. No indication we're blaming them."

"No good cop, bad cop?" Monroe pouted. "I was looking forward to being the bad cop."

Hannah laughed at the idea of her lovely friend convincing anyone that she was tough law enforcement. "Maybe you should promise to sing for them if they are forthcoming."

"I'll sing if they sing."

Grinning at the pun, Hannah asked, "Where did all this energy come from?"

"It's the buzz I get from performing. The last couple days of rehearsals have been really invigorating. So much of life on the road is lonely. It's been a blessing to spend time playing and catching up with friends who share my passion for music. I think these festivals are even more entertaining for the performers than for the audience. It's like one big family reunion."

Hannah made a mental note to revisit the lonely road comment. First she wanted to focus on Monroe's optimistic description. "How does all the feuding fit in with the idea of a happy family reunion?"

Monroe quickly glanced over at her before turning her eyes back to the road. "What do you mean? What feud? Are you talking about Grandpa Eddie and Ward? I think that's old news, water under the bridge."

Hannah wasn't so sure, but she let it go for the moment. "Do you know anything about the feud between Ward's family and the Hughes family?"

Monroe scrunched up her face, apparently digging into her memory. "That sort of rings a bell. Like I might have heard mention of it, but it's certainly nothing major. Why do you ask?"

She debated revealing what she'd learned, but Monroe wasn't a suspect, so there was no reason not to share her findings. Maybe her friend would recall some crucial detail. "I looked at the police file, and your grandpa is right. There was very little investigation done when the mandolin went missing. When I did my own searching, I discovered that the newspaper reporter who was ostensibly in town to cover the festival in '76 was actually a member of a family that had been feuding with Ward's family for generations."

"Well, if it was Ward's family, that would explain why I'm not familiar with it. But why would that lead to Grandpa Eddie's mandolin being stolen? He didn't have anything to do with that feud."

Hannah shrugged. "I have no proof that this journalist was involved, but I need to investigate every lead. The rift between Eddie and Ward broke up the band, so stealing the mandolin would have served her purpose—if she had such a purpose, that is."

"I guess," Monroe responded, but Hannah could tell she wasn't convinced. They pulled into the storage company parking lot and climbed out of the car. "Who's taking lead here?"

"Why don't you explain who you are and what was in storage, then remind them it was delivered to the library last week? I can pick up from there."

Monroe agreed, and they crossed to the entrance of a small trailer with a sign denoting it as the main office.

Inside, the trailer was a makeshift office so small that when Hannah and Monroe entered, they found themselves face-to-face with a young man at a desk. He was chewing gum and playing a video game of some kind. He didn't appear to notice them until Monroe cleared her throat.

He looked up as if surprised to see humans standing before him.

"Hello, I'd like to speak to someone about goods put in storage several decades ago," Monroe said to him.

"What do you want to know?"

"I guess for starters, who I'd need to talk to about it."

He made a point of looking around the trailer, then turned back to Monroe. "Looks like that would be me. What do you want?"

Monroe dangled the receipt. "My grandmother had your storage company pack up some belongings decades ago, and I have some questions about them."

He didn't look at the receipt but asked, "Do you have a key?"

"No."

He shrugged. "Not much I can do to help without a key."

"You don't need a key to answer questions."

Monroe's voice was deceptively sweet, but Hannah caught an underlying bite. What had happened to the Monroe who'd been laughing a short time ago? Suddenly Hannah could see the tension that had been building in her friend all week reach a breaking point.

Hannah stepped in to defuse the situation. "I'm sorry for the confusion. We don't have a key because the boxes are no longer here. They were delivered to the Blackberry Valley Library last week."

The man looked genuinely confused. "Then what do you want from me?"

Monroe sputtered at her side, but Hannah briefly rested a hand on her arm to calm her.

"We were helping unpack the crates at the library and encountered something unusual," Hannah explained. "That is why we wanted to speak with whoever is in charge here."

"Ma'am, what you see is what you get. There's nobody here but me."

Hannah raised an eyebrow. "You're a one-man operation?"

He folded his arms and leaned back in his chair. "It's a family business. I'm the manager. I have a crew that handles packing and storage."

"Who would have been sitting in your chair forty or so years ago?"

He straightened almost imperceptibly. "That would have been my granddad, but if you're aiming to talk to him, you're out of luck. He passed on years ago."

That was a possibility she hadn't considered. Hannah sighed in frustration. She should have, just like she probably should have left this part of the investigation to the sheriff. It was a long shot, at best, to think the current staff knew anything about what had happened in the eighties. Colin would be able to subpoena records if he decided there was cause.

Hannah peered at the name embroidered on his shirt. "Thanks for your help, Cal."

He made a face. "So you're just going to leave without telling me why you came?"

Hannah was almost tempted to tell him, just to see his reaction, but she knew better. If Colin did need to follow up, it would be better if she hadn't shown their hand. "As I said, there was something unusual in the box, but since you can't help me with that, I guess we're done. Have a nice rest of your day." Hannah placed her hand on Monroe's arm again and led her out.

They'd barely made it out of the trailer before Monroe stopped. "We didn't get any answers. Why are we leaving?"

"You heard him. His grandfather is dead. Cal can't be any older than twenty-five, so he wasn't even alive back then. No sense getting into it with him." Hannah could feel Monroe's arm trembling beneath her hand. "Are you okay to drive?"

"I am."

Monroe squared her shoulders, and for a moment Hannah feared she would turn and charge back into the trailer. "Let's get back in the car. We really should have left this to the sheriff. I hoped maybe the man managing the facility now would know something, but that really was unlikely." Hannah had been hoping for anything to help solve this mystery because she didn't want to let her friend down.

"The mandolin disappeared years before my nana hired this company, so they probably had nothing to do with it," Monroe acknowledged as they climbed into her convertible. "I guess I wanted an answer to appear out of nowhere."

Hannah agreed but she didn't give voice to the one question regarding the storage company that lingered in her mind. Why had Beverly chosen to put everything in storage ten years after the last festival? She'd said it was because she knew there was no hope of the festival being revived, but shouldn't that have been apparent right away? Why have things packed up by a storage company ten years later? Had she been trying to hide something?

Hannah sat in silence, not liking the direction her thoughts were taking. The idea of Beverly hiding something made no sense. If she were responsible for hiding the mandolin, why would she have offered to loan the memorabilia to the library?

Hannah mulled it over. There was one other possibility to consider. Beverly was getting older. Was it possible she'd known the mandolin was in there and had seized an opportunity to make sure it got back to Eddie? The thoughts whirled in Hannah's head, none of them providing answers, and none reflecting well on Beverly. But would any of them explain her anxiety and her request that Hannah come to her if she found anything?

A sniffle from Monroe drew Hannah from her reverie. She glanced over at her friend, whose shoulders shook as she fought back tears. How had she gone from fury to this in the time Hannah had been deep in thought? Were her thoughts running parallel to Hannah's? Was she also worried about Beverly's involvement?

"Monroe, what's wrong?" she asked gently.

Her friend let out a sob. "Everything. My whole life."

Chapter Fourteen

That was the last response Hannah had been expecting. "What do you mean? You've got a great career, you—" Hannah stopped speaking when she realized her words had caused a fresh wave of tears.

Her phone started to buzz, but she ignored it. "Monroe, talk to me. I know it's been a while since we were close friends, but you can tell me anything." The phone buzzed again with an incoming text.

"Go ahead and check that," Monroe said as she wiped away her tears and started the engine. "I'm fine."

"It's Lacy, inviting us to lunch. It's okay if you don't want to go. She'll understand."

Monroe sniffed again. "No, we should go. Will you give me directions to the farm?"

"If you're sure." Hannah's questions were multiplying. Between the fruitless visit to the storage facility and Monroe dissolving into tears, she was at loose ends. Maybe lunch in a friendly, peaceful setting would help. She sent a quick text back to Lacy and then pointed Monroe in the right direction.

For the rest of the trip, Monroe seemed back to her normal self. By the time they pulled up the lane to Bluegrass Hollow Farm, she was excited to see Lacy's home in daylight. "It's so pretty here. Lacy's done a great job with it. I love the black shutters against the white farmhouse. It's such a great contrast."

The farm was like a second home to Hannah, but now she saw it through Monroe's eyes. Eyes that were becoming glassy with emotion again. "Are you okay?"

Monroe nodded and fixed a bright smile on her face as she left the car and led Hannah up the path to the door. Lacy welcomed them in and gave Monroe a tour of the first floor, ending in her spacious kitchen. They chattered happily about everything from the festival to Lacy's baby while they ate a delicious lunch of egg salad made from farm-fresh eggs on croissants from Sweet Caroline's. Lacy also served homemade coleslaw and potato chips, with mixed berries and cream for dessert.

When they finished, Lacy offered to take Monroe on an outside tour. "You've heard all about my farm, but are you ready to meet my chickens, Hennifer, Eggatha, and Rocky?"

Monroe, who had lost all semblance of sadness over lunch, hopped up from her chair. "I'd love to. Hannah told me you have horses too."

"That's right. Stunner, Misty, and Razzle Dazzle. Are you coming to see them, Hannah?"

Hannah shook her head. "Go on without me. I need to call Colin and update him on how our visit to the storage company went. Maybe I'll catch up with you."

Lacy grabbed a sun hat from a hook by the door and led Monroe out through the back. Hannah immediately took out her phone and placed a call to the sheriff's office. Vanessa told her Colin was in a lunch meeting, so Hannah left a message for him to return her call as soon as possible. She lifted her glass of water and sipped as she debated following Lacy and Monroe. It might be nice to give them a little time on their own, free from the mystery.

She could focus on little else though, so she pulled her notebook from her bag and opened it to the action plan she'd made. She could do a little research into Maureen Hughes on her phone while she waited for the sheriff to call back.

After a few false starts with general searches, Hannah turned her attention to the book title. She typed in *Out of the Holler* and finally found what she was looking for. The book was out of print, but back in the 1990s, Maureen Hughes Wright had written a book by that name.

Hannah found an author page, which confirmed that the journalist who had written about the festival in the *Chronicle* had climbed the social ladder. She'd married a prominent Philadelphia man named Baxter Wright, who was unfortunately killed in action not long after their daughter was born. More research revealed that Maureen Hughes Wright now lived in Nashville.

Hannah found a phone number for her and, without allowing herself time to think better of it, placed a call.

"Hello?" The voice was hesitant but clear.

Hannah wished she'd taken a moment to figure out what she would say, but then she decided to tell the truth. Or rather, as much of the truth as she thought the sheriff would be comfortable with her sharing. "Good afternoon. My name is Hannah Prentiss. I'm on the Blackberry Valley Bluegrass Festival Committee, and I was hoping to reach Mrs. Maureen Hughes Wright."

"This is Maureen. I thought that festival was a thing of the past."

"It was," Hannah confirmed. "But the son of the original promoter decided to bring it back for the fiftieth anniversary of the final show."

"Well, I'll be. That's interesting news, but why are you calling me?"

"I was doing some research on previous festivals, and your name kept surfacing as the journalist who covered the festival for *The Blackberry Valley Chronicle*."

"That I did. Covering the festival was the smartest thing I ever did. It was my ticket to fame, if you will."

"I understand you were invited to join a large metropolitan newspaper as a result of those stories in the *Chronicle*."

"I was indeed. But I worked very hard for years before my apparent overnight success." Maureen cleared her throat. "If you already know about my articles, why are you calling? Is it because the mandolin turned up last week?"

Right. That had been published in the newspaper too. "The thing is, Mrs. Wright, I tried to read your articles, but online you can only see a headline, so I went to the *Chronicle* to view the archives. The editor is a friend, and he agreed to let me read the old issues, but when we went to pull them out of storage, the shelves were bare. The storage bins were missing."

"They were probably just misplaced." The woman's tone couldn't be described as anything other than complacent.

Maureen's complete lack of concern roused Hannah's curiosity. Didn't she care that her work had gone missing? Of course it was from a long time ago, but she'd basically admitted those articles had been her ticket out of town.

Could she have something to do with the back issues being missing? Was there something in them that incriminated her? That seemed like a stretch. Plenty of people had already read the articles, so surely anything suspicious in them would have been caught by someone else long ago. And the idea of a woman aged eighty-something sneaking into the *Chronicle's* basement was ludicrous.

But none of that changed the fact that Maureen Hughes was her prime suspect.

"Since I can't read the articles themselves, would you be willing to let me come speak with you about your memories of the festival?" Hannah asked.

Silence lasted long enough that Hannah was confident her request would be rejected.

At last, Maureen replied, "I can't imagine what you could possibly gain from talking to me, but I'm always happy to have visitors. Life is a lot lonelier now than it was when I was that young reporter."

Hannah wasn't sure if she was more surprised that she'd asked or that her request had been granted, but she eagerly set a time for the next morning. "We have a lovely bakery here in town. Is there anything I can bring as a thank-you?"

"Being that it's Blackberry Valley, I don't suppose there's a chance they do a jam cake? I always did love a blackberry jam cake."

"They do indeed, and it's a good one. I'll be sure to pick one up on my way in the morning. Thank you so much for agreeing to see me."

"I'm looking forward to the visit."

Hannah disconnected the call, and her heart felt lighter. Finally she had something that might hold some promise, though she hated to think that this sweet-voiced, cake-loving woman could possibly be connected to the thefts.

As she sat there waiting for the sheriff to call, or Monroe and Lacy to return, Hannah recalled that she'd intended to look up some photos from the old festivals. Hoping she was on a roll, she opened her phone's browser and started searching for bluegrass festivals.

Surprisingly, the first result that popped up was an old video from the very first Blackberry Valley festival. It was grainy and short, with scratchy audio, but it was more than she'd expected to find.

The video had been recorded during the daytime and gave a good view of the same field she'd walked across last night. At the far end was a simple wooden platform stage with a cloth awning, much less elaborate than the one that was currently under construction. Onstage, a group of men in suits played instruments for a crowd gathered on blankets on the grass. Children played and danced in front of the stage. Families enjoyed picnics as they listened to the music.

Hannah tried to zoom in to see who was performing, but the video quality wasn't good enough, and the stage just became a blur. She clicked to another video, this one dated 1969.

She immediately noticed how much the festival had grown. Not only was the crowd larger, but the stage had increased in size and design. The cloth awning had been replaced by an actual roof over the performers. The caption under the video read, *Blackberry Mountain Boys close out the show with a round of gospel and bluegrass medleys.*

Hannah pressed play. Goose bumps prickled her arms as she listened, for the first time, to the actual sound of Eddie Conley and his band performing. When the video ended, she just sat there grinning. She'd always been impressed with Eddie's singing, but his skill on the mandolin was undeniable, especially supported by the other talented musicians in the group. She recalled Beverly talking about the close bond between Eddie and Ward. It had been so obvious in this performance—like they were born to play together.

Her smile slipped. They'd lost that friendship. It had been strained by an ongoing argument, then broken by the theft of the mandolin. She wondered how Ward had dealt with the loss all these years. He'd gone on to have a successful career, but he'd had to face the repercussions of Eddie's accusation. She knew Eddie regretted that.

Maybe if she could solve this mystery, they could regain a little of what they'd lost. Would Ward be open to that? Hannah decided to visit him and find out, plus see if he had any ideas about who might have taken the instrument.

Hannah looked back to the video and made a note of who had posted it. It would be such fun to include old footage in the library exhibit. Maybe she could contact the person and see if there were any others. Maybe one of them would hold a clue that could help solve the mystery.

Her phone buzzed, and she was happy to see the sheriff's number. "Colin, thanks for returning my call." She quickly filled him in on her meeting with Cal at the storage company. "It's not likely that he's hiding anything, since the storage company got involved a decade after the mandolin and money vanished. I'd love to hear your take on it if you decide to pay them a visit, though."

"It would be a good idea for me to drop by and see if his story stays the same. I'll be in touch. Good work, Hannah."

"Thanks, Sheriff." Hannah disconnected the call and found another video to watch. When she saw the date, it hit her that someone had recorded the final day of the festival. Could there be any clues in here?

Before Hannah could hit play, she heard Monroe and Lacy chatting as they approached the house. It sounded like Lacy's farm animals had kept Monroe's spirits high. Would seeing the video raise them more—or would it spoil her mood by reminding her of the mystery?

"You two look like you've been having fun," Hannah said as they entered the house laughing. "But Lacy, you should sit down and let me get you some water. We wouldn't want you to get dehydrated."

Lacy rolled her eyes. "Why does everyone act like I am unable to take care of myself? In a couple months, I'll be responsible for me and this baby."

"It's because we all love you so," Hannah insisted, but as she said the words, she noticed the crestfallen expression that had come over Monroe's face.

Lacy noticed too. "Monroe, what's wrong? Please tell me you're not also worried about me."

Monroe looked down. "No, just a little jealous. Of both of you."

Was this what had been bothering Monroe all day? Hannah finished filling two water glasses and brought them to the table for each of her friends. "Back in the car, you said your life was a mess. You're going through a tough time with your grandparents and the festival. It's normal to feel emotional. Do you want to talk about it? Maybe we can help."

Monroe took a long drink of the water, and Hannah wasn't sure if she was that thirsty or simply stalling. At last, she said, "It's not that. Well, not just that. It's something that's been weighing on me, but since I've been home, it's been worse."

Hannah and Lacy sat quietly, waiting for her to continue in her own time.

Monroe turned to Hannah. "Remember when Nana was telling us how she was considered a suspect because she was unhappy about the amount of time Grandpa Eddie was spending on the road?"

Hannah nodded.

"That felt really familiar to me. It's a crossroads a lot of musicians face. How do you weigh the price of success? Starting out, the love of music carries you through long, lonely days on the road. The adrenaline rush of a performance makes you forget all the downtime, the travel time, the alone time." She paused for another sip of water. "Don't get me wrong. I love my career. I am so grateful that I have a chance to make a living doing what I love, and that I get to bring joy to others while I'm doing it."

"But it's no longer enough?" Lacy asked softly.

A tear slid down Monroe's cheek as she nodded. "And the guilt makes it worse. So many people would give anything to have what I have. But I want what you have."

Hannah grabbed a pack of tissues from her bag and handed them to her friend.

Monroe wiped her eyes and continued. "I'm not getting any younger, and I've spent my whole life pursuing my career. I get to perform and I have all these fans who enjoy the music, but look at you, Lacy. You're running this farm and you're about to become a mom. And, Hannah, you're running your own restaurant. You're engaged and planning a wedding, not to mention solving mysteries." She sniffled. "I've got a great career that I really do appreciate, but at the end of the day, I go home alone. That would be fine if a career was all I wanted, but it's not."

Hannah and Lacy exchanged a glance. They both knew it wasn't easy. Hannah hoped sharing her experience would help her friend. She reached across the table and covered Monroe's hand with her own. "Lacy doesn't know this, but when I first came back to Blackberry Valley, I was a little jealous of her too."

Lacy and Monroe both looked surprised.

Hannah continued. "Several months ago, Lacy was telling me she was glad I was back where I belonged, and I agreed. I said something about sometimes you know you made the right decision. Lacy replied that was exactly how she felt when Neil proposed." Hannah shot a smile at her friend, who nodded as if she were remembering the conversation. "I had to fight a twinge of jealousy in that moment. Here I was, riding high on the first successful months of fulfilling my lifelong dream to open my restaurant, and I was jealous of my best friend because she was married. So I know exactly what you're saying. We can't stop our hearts from wanting what they want."

"What did you do with the feelings?" Monroe asked quietly.

"I prayed about it. I reminded myself that if it was God's will, I would find the right person and have that life too. Then I concentrated on appreciating the gift of having my own restaurant and making the most of the talents God gave me."

Monroe's lower lip trembled.

Hannah squeezed her hand. "Please don't take that as a lecture. That was not the only time I had to fight off those feelings. Even after I started dating Liam, we had to work hard to figure out how to balance our careers and our hope to build a life together. It's gotten easier because we're committed to each other and our future, but we know it's going to continue to be a balancing act." She shrugged.

"That's life. I know it's harder for you because you're never in one place for very long, but maybe you can think of it as more opportunities to meet the right person."

Monroe gave her a wry smile. "In other words, trust God's timing."

"Easier said than done. I know."

Monroe's expression softened. "Thank you both. Just being able to talk about it with you does make it easier. My mom and I share everything, but it's hard to talk to her about this since my dad died when they were so newly married. She could have remarried. She had lots of would-be suitors over the years, but she was always a one-man woman."

"You know," Hannah said, as something clicked in her mind. "You have something in common with my chief suspect."

"You have a suspect?" Monroe asked.

"Yes, but it's only a feeling for now," Hannah cautioned. She explained her thoughts about Maureen Hughes, from the missing files to the family feud. "I have no proof, but I am going to visit her in Nashville tomorrow. Anyone want to join me?"

"Yes, please," Lacy said at once. "Anything for a change of scenery."

"I still don't understand what we have in common. Do you mean the feud?" Monroe asked.

"Sure, but that wasn't what I meant. When I spoke to Maureen, she mentioned that her husband was killed in action shortly after they were married, when her daughter was young. Which means you actually have more in common with her daughter."

Monroe made a face. "I hope that doesn't mean I have to forgive her mother." She hung her head. "Okay, I hate that I said that. It's just when I think of all the pain that the theft of the mandolin caused, I'm not in a very forgiving frame of mind."

"I understand. But remember, I only said Maureen was a *suspect*. I don't have any proof other than the feud and the missing newspaper files."

"I would love to go with you, but unfortunately, I'll be in rehearsals all morning. I expect you to call with all the details."

"We will. Do you want to hear what else I discovered while you were playing with the chickens?"

Monroe and Lacy laughed, just as Hannah had hoped.

She opened her phone and pulled up the videos. "Prepare yourself for a trip back to 1960s and '70s fashion."

Lacy squealed in delight. "I've seen photos of my mother in bell-bottoms like those. And the cutoffs. Look at their hair."

Monroe's focus was on her grandfather and Ward. "They were so young and so happy together."

"That's exactly what I thought when I watched it, Monroe."

Monroe slapped her hand against her forehead. "I can't believe I didn't think of this before. Grandpa Eddie has videos of the festivals. I'm not sure how exactly we'd play them, and I don't know how good the quality is because I was never allowed to see them. Apparently, it was too hard on him to remember. Seeing this video, I can understand why. He lost so much more than the mandolin."

"Your grandpa wants the mystery solved," Hannah said. "Maybe he'll let me see them."

"It can't hurt to ask," Monroe said. "And if he agrees, I'll ask one of the festival techs for a suggestion on how to play them."

"Good." Monroe's words about Eddie's loss had deepened Hannah's resolve. "I need to solve this mystery so we can try to reunite your grandfather and Ward."

Blackberry Valley
June 1970

Beverly Conley and Peggy Burton carried pitchers of lemonade and bowls of snacks out to the back lawn where Eddie and Ward sat with their manager, Martin Lowe, and his wife, Shelby. Arthur White and his wife, Ellie, were just arriving, so Beverly went to welcome them.

Once everyone was settled, Eddie lifted his glass. "Here's to another amazing festival on the books."

The cheers were echoed by the toddlers playing on the grass. Eddie smiled at his daughter, Sandy, who spun in circles holding hands with Ward's son, Junior. Other than being onstage sharing his music, these quiet times with his music family were what brought him the greatest joy. He and Ward went all the way back to childhood, but Martin and Arthur had become like brothers after working together for half a decade.

Arthur sat forward in his chair. "I know you're happy with the way things are going, Eddie, but Martin, Ward, and I were talking about some changes for next year's festival."

Change wasn't a word Eddie much liked, and Beverly knew it. She whispered in his ear, "Just hear them out."

Eddie nodded. "Go on."

Martin spoke up. "I know you don't want to electrify your sound, and I'm not fool enough to push that. The last thing I'd want to do is cause friction between the duo that pays my bills. But Arthur has some ideas to make the festival bigger and better. It's been great fun keeping it small, with only the Blackberry Mountain Boys and some other local groups performing, but festivals are taking off across the country. We think adding more acts and some jam sessions would bring in larger crowds."

"You've built enough of a reputation that I think I can get some big acts to join you," Arthur added. "Bigger names and more days will generate more money for all of us."

"I like the sound of that," Ward said.

Eddie sat back against the chair. It was hard to let go of the small-town feel he'd loved about this festival, but this wasn't about him. Ward, Arthur, and Martin all had families to support. If expanding the festival could postpone the debate about amplifying their sound, then he could get on board. "Bev?"

She smiled that private smile that always made his heart beat a little faster. "I think you should do it. Let more people hear the magical sound of Eddie and his mandolin."

"You heard the lady, Arthur." Eddie lifted his glass again. "Here's to bigger and better."

Chapter Fifteen

Monroe dropped Hannah off at the Hot Spot door before heading off to pick up her mother from the airport, but she promised to let Hannah know as soon as she had an answer about the videos.

Hannah hurried inside and glanced at the time, calculating how long she had before she had to get to work in the kitchen. But when she walked through the dining room, she noticed that everything was already set to open. And she could hear whistling in the kitchen. She pushed through the swinging door and stopped dead at the sight of Jacob, in complete chef regalia, whistling a bluegrass tune.

He stopped when he saw her, and she raised her hands to applaud. "My chef has skills beyond the kitchen. Who knew? Maybe you should join the next jam session."

"I will if you will."

Hannah stopped clapping and turned her hands outward in a show of surrender. "My talents tend more toward mystery solving."

"Speaking of which, how's that going? Have you figured out who stole the mandolin yet?"

"No. But I'm going to visit one of the suspects in the morning." Hannah glanced around the kitchen. Aside from the appetizers Jacob was currently working on, everything appeared to be prepped for dinner. "How long have you been here?"

"A while. I wanted to try out a new recipe that requires long, low cooking, so I did the other prep work while it was on."

Hannah understood that reasoning. It was the kind of thing she would do. "Is there anything for me to do?"

Jacob reached behind him to pull down a list he'd attached to the wall. "We've been going through produce more rapidly than usual, so I made you a list of things we'll be low on if the crowds keep up and we don't increase our order."

"I'll see to that now. Have we heard anything about tonight?"

"I haven't checked the messages, but if the way the phone has been ringing is any indication, I'd guess news about the jam session got around."

"I hadn't even considered that. I'll check the messages. Call me if you need anything."

"Sounds like you've had a busy morning sleuthing. Why don't you give yourself an hour or so to unwind before tonight? There's nothing more to be done down here."

"What did I ever do to deserve you?"

"I don't know, but it must have been good, huh?" Jacob grinned, and Hannah laughed as she headed back out of the kitchen.

She quickly placed her order and then checked the phone line. Her eyes bugged at the number of calls. She didn't want to mess with Elaine's system, so she grabbed a pad of paper and wrote names and numbers as she listened. The third call was a hang-up. Maybe a wrong number, or maybe someone calling back to see if anyone answered. Hannah recorded another group of reservations, including someone calling on behalf of the festival performers, before she encountered another hang-up. That seemed strange, but she'd have to ask Elaine how common it was before she knew whether it was something to be concerned about.

Hannah left the list for Elaine to enter in her system and then headed upstairs. She'd love to take a nap, but there wasn't enough time for her mind and body to wind down before she would have to report back downstairs. Instead, she put on water for tea and sent a message to Liam to check in. WE'RE EXPECTING ANOTHER FULL HOUSE TONIGHT. STOP BY IF YOU CAN.

He replied immediately. AS LONG AS THERE ARE NO EMERGENCIES, I'LL BE IN LATER. LOVE YOU.

The message warmed her heart. It had been less than twenty-four hours since she'd seen him, but that felt like too long. Hannah sent back some heart emojis as the kettle began to whistle.

She fixed her tea, then settled down at her computer and pulled up the video she hadn't had a chance to watch at Lacy's, the one from the last day of the festival in '76. Maybe on the larger screen she'd be able to spot a clue.

First, she let the video play all the way through to get a good sense of it. As she watched, she was struck by how difficult it was to hear the music over the noise of the crowd. That realization gave her a better understanding of both sides of the debate about amplifying their sound. She definitely understood Ward's position, because the people in the back certainly couldn't hear very well in a crowd this size.

The problem was, she also understood Eddie's side. It was the unique and intimate sound of bluegrass that made it special. Would that be lost with amplification? What really stood out to her was that there really was no middle ground. Were Ward and Eddie fated to break up, even if the mandolin had never been stolen?

As she watched the video a second time, Hannah noticed something new. About midway through, Eddie and Ward stepped off for a break, and some new performers took their places. She enlarged the screen to see if she could recognize anyone. This looked like a younger generation. Only one person appeared vaguely familiar, but it was too blurry to place the face until the guitarist announced the replacements. "On mandolin, we have Junior Burton."

His voice droned on, but Hannah stayed focused on the younger version of the man she'd met in her restaurant last night. Junior couldn't have been more than ten years old in the video. Interesting that he was playing mandolin, since she distinctly remembered that last night he had been on bass.

How kind it was that Eddie and Ward had encouraged younger musicians. Before long, Ward and Eddie joined them onstage, and the music turned even more lively. Hannah felt a twang of envy for the people in the audience. How she would have loved the chance to see and hear this performance in person. If she solved the mystery, maybe she could still see a reunion.

Blackberry Valley
June 1973

"Look at the size of this crowd!" Eddie was dumbfounded. It was only the first day of this year's festival, and already the audience overflowed the campground. "Arthur said if we changed our approach, more people would come, and each year they do. It just blows my mind."

"We'd have even bigger crowds if you'd agree to amplifying our sound," Ward countered. "The people in the back can barely hear."

Eddie lightly strummed his mandolin. He was tired of fighting over this. "Maybe we should get down in the middle instead of being way up here. All you keep talking about is amplifying our sound, playing for larger crowds. Why? What's wrong with keeping it smaller, more like family? That's how we started out."

"There's not enough money in that. Eddie, I'm tired of being on the road all the time. Fifty-two weeks a year, three or four shows a week playing small venues and back rooms, and still not making enough to eke out a living."

"There's nothing wrong with the living we earn unless you're getting too big for your Kentucky britches and care more about fancy cars than your music."

Ward's face grew red, and he clenched his fist at his side as he glared at his lifelong friend. "If we're going low, then I'll just say that maybe you should care a little less about your music and a little more about your wife and daughter."

Eddie stepped toward him, jaw firm and eyes burning. "You leave Bev and Sandy out of this."

"You mean like you're leaving them out of your life?" Ward's voice softened as he let go of his anger. "Speaking as a friend, it's time you woke up and paid attention to something other than that mandolin." When he got no reply, Ward shook his head and headed back to the trailers.

Eddie sat on the edge of the stage and stared out over the crowd. He didn't want to pay heed to Ward's warning, but the words hit close to home.

"Mr. Conley, sir?" A young voice pulled Eddie from his musings. The tow-headed boy standing below the stage was gazing up at him the way he'd once looked at the great Bill Monroe.

"Hello, young fella. What can I do for you?"

"Would you sign my program?"

Eddie's mood was no match for the youngster's enthusiasm. He noticed the mandolin tucked under the boy's arm. "You play?"

The kid nodded his head vigorously.

"Then come on up and show me."

The boy's face lit with excitement, but he carefully set his instrument on the stage before scrambling up beside it with Eddie lending him a hand.

"What can you play?"

"'Rocky Top'!"

Eddie chuckled. "An Osbornes fan, are you? The brothers are good friends of mine. Okay, let's see what you can do."

The boy began to pick the first few notes, but Eddie stopped him and gently adjusted his hold and finger placement. The boy played a few notes and grinned. "That's good."

Eddie picked up his own mandolin again. "So, let's jam." He started the song and waited for the boy to catch up. Before long, they had gathered a crowd, clapping and singing along.

When the song ended, Eddie joined the crowd in applauding the young boy. "I have to go get ready for our next set, but thanks for joining me." He signed the program and headed backstage, his heart lighter. This was the reason he would never give in to Ward's demands. This personal connection was everything he'd ever wanted.

Chapter Sixteen

By eight o'clock Wednesday night, the Hot Spot was hopping even more than the previous night. Elaine claimed she'd had to turn down dozens of reservation requests. That news saddened Hannah. If only there was a way to include everyone. At least they would all have a chance to hear the music at the festival.

Hannah was run off her feet between helping Jacob plate meals and lending a hand when Raquel or Dylan seemed overwhelmed. In between, she visited all the tables, greeting the locals, welcoming visitors, and thanking everyone for coming.

Musicians and crew from the festival arrived for two different seatings, for which Hannah was grateful. The musicians came about an hour before closing, and once again they had their instruments with them. But they also brought big appetites, so she hurried to the kitchen to assist Jacob. He was ready with his barbecue special.

When the last dishes had been cleared and the tables rearranged, the musicians brought out their instruments and tuned up. Hannah glanced at her phone, but there was no message from Liam. Hopefully there hadn't been any more fires at the campgrounds.

She joined Elaine, who appeared exhausted and exhilarated at the same time. "Are you holding up okay?"

Elaine nodded. "It's been fantastic. Not that I could manage crowds like this every night, but just for festival week, I'll take it. What an amazing experience, to end with a private concert each night. Even these tired toes are tapping," she added, pointing down at her feet.

Hannah could empathize with aching feet. And it was only Wednesday. "Let's find a seat."

More diners hung around even though the kitchen was closed, but Hannah was still able to find an empty table. Since Raquel was already squeezed in next to Marshall, Hannah waved Jacob and Dylan over for a well-deserved break.

The jam session energized everyone, as the talented musicians played some favorites and then took requests from their audience. Although the playing went on past their normal closing hour, Hannah didn't have the heart to shut them down. She told her staff they were free to leave, but no one wanted to break up the fun.

When Junior finally noticed the time, he called for a final song. Once everyone had sung along to "Blue Moon of Kentucky," Junior came over to Hannah to apologize for overstaying their welcome.

"No apology is necessary," she assured him. "We all chose to stay because we were enjoying your music so much. It's been a treat. We're going to be sad when the festival is over." She glanced at the instrument he'd set aside before joining her. "When did you start playing bass?"

He smiled broadly. "When I was just a kid. I learned on a three-quarters scale bass and never stopped."

"What made you switch from the mandolin?"

"I didn't play the mandolin. When my dad was in the band, that was Mr. Eddie's role, and no one I knew could play the mandolin like Eddie Conley. I would have been too afraid to try to follow in his footsteps."

The guitarist called to Junior, so he made his excuses, thanked them all again, and left before Hannah could ask him about the video. Could she have been wrong? She certainly would never have been rude enough to call him out on it in front of the crowd, but something about his answer rang false. She'd have to look at the video again. Or she could show a screenshot to Eddie. She didn't want to force him to watch the video, but he'd certainly recognize the boy and remember whether Ward's son had played the mandolin at his shows.

There was still no word from Liam. Hannah knew she wouldn't rest until she heard from him, so after the basic cleanup was done, she shooed everyone else off home and finished up herself. She was unloading the dishwasher when she heard a light knock at the back door just as her phone dinged with an incoming message from Liam.

Saw your lights on, so I came for a good-night kiss.

Hannah whispered a prayer of thanks for his safety and hurried to unlock the back door. She would have to get used to nights like these as a firefighter's wife, so she shrugged off her worries as she opened the door and welcomed him. Rising up on tiptoe to give him the requested kiss, she murmured, "I missed you."

Liam held her close for a minute. "I missed you too, and I'm sorry I didn't make the show. We got called in to assist on a fire outside Glasgow."

"Everything okay?"

"Yes. An abandoned shed set on fire. It wouldn't have required extra help if not for the winds blowing sparks. But all is well now. The local truck will stay on scene overnight."

"At least it wasn't more trouble at the festival grounds. That reminds me, did you get a chance to talk to your granddad?"

Liam shook his head. "I called this afternoon, but they said he was napping. He called while I was out at the fire tonight, but I missed it. I promise I'll catch up with him tomorrow." He gave her another kiss, then settled on a stool. "How was your day? Any progress solving the mystery?"

Hannah frowned. "Not really. Just more questions. Let me show you something." She came around beside him, pulled out her phone, and opened the video, pausing when it reached the younger pickers. "Does this remind you of anyone?"

Liam squinted at the phone. "It's a kid."

"Yes, but I think he looks pretty much the same now."

Liam studied it a little longer. "I'd say the man we met last night, but he was playing bass then."

"I knew I wasn't imagining it," Hannah said in triumph. "I asked him tonight about when he switched from mandolin to bass, and he told me he never played the mandolin."

Liam grinned. "I bet that shot him to the top of your suspect list."

"It might have. I'm going to ask Eddie about it first because he should know the truth." She made a face. "And Lacy and I are heading to Nashville tomorrow morning to meet with the newspaper reporter. Maureen was my number one suspect until I chatted with her. She seemed so forthcoming and friendly. But she wouldn't be the first criminal to fool people, so I'll reserve judgment for now."

"Seems wise. If you're heading to Nashville early, I shouldn't be keeping you awake. I just didn't want to head home without a good-night kiss."

Hannah beamed and gave him another. "You can always keep me awake for that."

By the next morning, Hannah was wishing she'd gone to sleep a little earlier, but even after Liam left, she'd struggled to quiet her mind. She'd finally put on some gospel bluegrass background music to lull herself to sleep. The next thing she knew, her alarm was ringing. Hannah yawned and hit snooze, grateful that she'd picked up the cake from Sweet Caroline's yesterday so she could steal a few more minutes of sleep.

When the alarm sounded the second time, Hannah dragged herself out of bed and into the shower. The hot water worked its magic. Lacy had promised to bring breakfast and coffee for their trip, so all Hannah had to do was get dressed and head to Bluegrass Hollow Farm.

Lacy looked even more exhausted than Hannah felt.

"Late night?" Hannah asked her.

"Rough one. Baby was playing soccer all night. I think my ribs were the goal post." Lacy set an insulated bag on the floor of the Subaru and handed Hannah a thermos of coffee. "Oops, wait. Wrong one. That's my decaf."

"If Liam and I are ever blessed with children, I don't know how I will survive without regular coffee," Hannah sympathized.

"You get used to it." Lacy waited until they were on the road before handing Hannah a breakfast sandwich. "So, should we talk about wedding plans, or where we're going today?"

Hannah groaned. "Let's stay focused on the mystery I can solve. Wedding planning is one I'm clueless about. At least with the mandolin, I've got some ideas."

Lacy laughed. "It's not that scary, I promise. Just time-consuming. How about you fill me in a little more on what to expect today?" She bit into her own hearty meal.

"I know I told you a bit about it yesterday, but since we have a long drive, I'll begin at the beginning. I want you to know everything I know so you can tell me if I'm way off base."

"Okay. Start with what first put Maureen on your radar. Should I give us a little bluegrass music to set the mood? I made a playlist—everything from Bill Monroe to Alison Krauss."

"That sounds perfect."

Lacy connected her phone to the Subaru, and soon "Every Time You Say Goodbye" was playing in the background.

Hannah began. "You asked what put her on my radar. I think it was when Jack Delaney took me down to the *Chronicle*'s basement so I could read the archives, and all the issues with Maureen's articles were missing."

"That would make me suspicious too, but it doesn't prove anything."

"Agreed. But then later that night at your house, Evangeline and Miriam were talking about the feud. I may have jumped to conclusions, but a member of a feuding family seems to have more motive than anyone else I've encountered thus far."

Rhiannon Giddens singing "Cluck Old Hen" popped up on the playlist, and Hannah burst into laughter. "You just couldn't resist, could you?"

Lacy grinned. "Hennifer chose that one. It's her favorite."

Hannah ate some of her sandwich as she pondered what to say next. "I guess I don't really have any other reason to suspect her, other than the circumstantial stuff. As a member of the press, she would have had easy access to just about anywhere on the festival grounds, and her presence wouldn't have roused any suspicions."

"True, but you're not convinced, are you? I hear a 'but' in your voice."

"That's why you're such a good partner," Hannah said. "The 'but' really surfaced when I spoke with her yesterday. She shrugged off the missing archives like it was no big deal—and maybe it's not. After all, so many people have already read the articles, so what would be the point of stealing them?"

"You haven't read them."

"No. I saw some previews online, but you couldn't click through to read the old articles."

"True, but you and Colin have reopened the investigation. Maybe she's afraid of someone seeing something today that they missed in the investigation back then."

Hannah mulled that over. "It's not a bad idea. Eddie told me the sheriff blew off the investigation, but if it was clear that Colin was reopening it, then maybe—" She broke off laughing.

"What's so funny?"

"Me. I'm getting carried away, thinking Maureen could have broken into the office and carried off those bins. She's eighty if she's a day."

"She could have had an accomplice. Hired someone to do it for her."

Hannah finished her breakfast. "I'd love that to be true so we can solve this, but even I think it's a stretch."

Lacy stubbornly lifted her chin. "Well, we're going to see her, so let's find out."

Chapter Seventeen

Hannah's first impression was that Maureen had done well for herself. The large house was in one of Nashville's more elegant neighborhoods and sat on a sizable lot. Lacy and Hannah parked, then entered through a gate and followed a short path to the front door. Lacy pressed the doorbell and stepped back to wait.

Within minutes the door was opened by a woman Hannah guessed to be in her late forties. She was dressed in a linen suit, and her hair was pulled up in a French knot. She pushed her glasses into her hair as she greeted them. "Good morning."

Hannah introduced herself and Lacy. "We're here to meet with Maureen Hughes Wright."

The woman smiled. "That's my mother. She's waiting for you in the solarium. I'm Hilary Wright."

She led them through a house that was decorated in an overly elegant style, apparently meant to prove Maureen had left her roots far behind. This home was figuratively as far from the holler as one could imagine, short of moving cross-country—as Hannah had done when she'd left for Los Angeles. That realization gave Hannah an idea about how to approach the conversation.

In the solarium, Hilary introduced them to her mother, a fashionably dressed woman reclining on a chaise lounge, and made her excuses. "I'll have the housekeeper bring you refreshments, but I have a client call to take. I hope to see you again before you leave."

"My daughter the lawyer," Maureen said as her daughter left. "She's been so good to me. I apologize for not rising to greet you. I recently had knee surgery and am not quite as mobile yet as I'd like."

"We are happy to meet you," Hannah responded. "I was thinking as we walked in that you and I have something in common. I, too, left Kentucky to make it big in the world." She shrugged and grinned. "Life in LA couldn't compete with the lure of home for me, though. I returned a year ago. Have you ever wanted to go back home?"

The pleasant expression vacated Maureen's face, replaced by a look of disgust. "Not even once. I have nothing against Kentucky, but Nashville is my home. I will never go back."

"You said that the festival in Blackberry Valley helped you make that move. Can you tell us what you remember about it?"

They were briefly interrupted when the housekeeper arrived with a coffee tray.

Once she had served them and left the room, Maureen took a sip of her coffee. "My life's blood. It's an addiction I developed as a young reporter and have never tried to kick. But you were asking about the festival." She slowly sipped her coffee as she dug back into her memories. "I'll admit, I wasn't thrilled to cover the festival at first. Hillbilly music, I called it. But Blackberry Valley was a lovely place, quite different from where I hailed from. Everyone was kind and welcoming. If I had to listen to bluegrass, it was fine as long as I got to stay there. For a time, I hoped I could swing a full-time job at *The Blackberry Valley Chronicle*."

This was news to Hannah. "What changed your mind?"

Maureen chuckled. "A better offer. That mandolin being stolen was tragic for Mr. Conley, but it changed my life for the better. I was a good writer, and the pieces I wrote about that lost mandolin tugged at people's heartstrings. As I told you, the columns were syndicated, and next thing I knew, I was getting job offers from around the country."

"I wish I could read those articles. It's so odd that they vanished."

Maureen tipped her head at a curious angle. "Why are you so interested?"

Lacy jumped in with an answer. "Because my friend can't stand unsolved puzzles. Eddie's mandolin showing up out of the blue has us all so curious to know about the time it was stolen. And of course the drama about the band breaking up."

"That was an unexpected bit of excitement." Maureen took another sip of coffee. "I understand curiosity. It's part of what made me such a good reporter. The mandolin wasn't the only thing stolen though. Did the money reappear too?"

Hannah shook her head. "Nope, that's still a mystery, as is what actually happened to the mandolin. Do you remember that the sheriff decided it must have been stolen by a fan?"

"He was a lazy man. I interviewed him. My impression was that his investigation was minimal and performative. Your coming here took more effort than he ever put into it." She tapped a manicured nail against her coffee cup. "You have me intrigued now too. I saved all my files from stories I worked on. Never knew when they might be useful. If you'd like, I can have Hilary bring them up from the basement. I'm happy to loan them to you if you promise to return them when you're done."

It was more than Hannah had expected from this trip. She eagerly agreed.

Later, as they drove toward the highway, Lacy was quiet.

"You don't think it's her, do you?" Hannah asked.

"Truthfully? No."

"Why not?"

Lacy shifted to face Hannah. "Do you think it's her?"

"No. But I want to see if our reasons match."

"Okay, but in no particular order because I haven't had time to really think it through."

Hannah laughed. "Go ahead. We've got a long drive to make sense of it all."

Lacy made a sheepish face. "First, I know criminals can be nice, but if she really is one, she fooled me. I liked her."

"Me too. She's funny and smart, and she seemed really kind. It's hard to imagine her stealing a mandolin and the profits. But, as I said to Liam last night, she wouldn't be the first criminal to fool people. I told him I was reserving judgment, but now that we've met her, I feel like it couldn't possibly be her. She was too generous and forthcoming. I mean, she offered us her files. They must contain more potentially incriminating evidence than anything in the newspaper articles themselves." Hannah gestured to the box in the back seat. "I guess I'll go through that before officially removing her from my short list of suspects."

"Oh, we've got a list? Who else is on it?"

"Maybe Ward's son." She explained about her conversation with Junior the previous night. "Why would he deny playing the mandolin?"

"Because he was ten and forgot he did?" Lacy suggested. "Are you even sure it was him?"

"Pretty sure. I'm going to show a screenshot to Eddie."

"Sounds like a plan. Any other suspects?"

Hannah shook her head slowly. "Not unless you count someone from the storage company. But as we discussed yesterday, given the timeline, that makes the least sense of anyone. So that brings me back to Maureen. Agreeable as she is now, she apparently was pretty desperate to make a name for herself as a budding journalist. Could she have done it to create the story that she then wrote about?"

"Oh, that's devious." Lacy rubbed her hands together. "You could be onto something. Think of her house. She obviously likes nice things."

"Yes, but that doesn't make her a thief. Lots of people like nice things."

"True, but didn't you hear it in her voice as she was talking? She was desperate to get out of Kentucky. And desperation makes people do things they usually wouldn't. Like stealing a mandolin and the profits."

Hannah bit her lower lip. "That's true."

Lacy shook her head. "The poor woman. Do you realize that over the course of this car ride alone we have declared her probably guilty but presumed her innocence, declared her innocent, but questioned the probability of that, and now tipped back toward guilty and given her selfish motives? I mean we could have assumed she had a sick mother who needed money for a treatment."

Hannah chuckled softly. "It's all so incredibly confusing. I have several viable suspects, but no legitimate evidence against any of them."

"You'll figure it out. You always do."

Hannah's shoulders sagged as she steered the car along the highway. "I appreciate the vote of confidence, but I'm really afraid I'm going to let Monroe and Eddie down."

Chapter Eighteen

Doubt continued to plague Hannah after she dropped Lacy off at the farm, so on an impulse she drove straight out to Eddie's house instead of heading into town. She'd like to know if this video really did show Junior before she had to face him again.

Beverly answered the door when Hannah knocked, and her worried expression all but broke Hannah's heart. "Good afternoon, Beverly. I promise not to bother you for long. I just wanted to show Eddie a photograph and see if he recognized the person."

A look that might have been panic passed over Beverly's face, reminding Hannah of the request to come to her first with any findings. Once again, Hannah was left to wonder what the elderly woman was hiding.

"He's out in the workshop, trying to fix his mandolin. I told him we could send it to a professional, but he's set on fixing it himself. I could look at the photo if you want."

"Okay." Hannah opened her phone and pulled up the photo she'd saved.

Immediately Beverly's face relaxed. She let out a breath and smiled fondly. "That's Junior. He was such a sweet boy. He loved playing with Eddie and Ward. If you still want to talk to Eddie, just head out back." She led Hannah to the back door and pointed to an old barn that had clearly been renovated not long before.

Hannah crossed the back lawn, relieved that Beverly had chosen not to accompany her. She preferred to keep the rest of the conversation between Eddie and herself.

As Hannah approached the doorway, she could see Eddie hunched over a table that was lit by sunshine and a set of spotlights. His mandolin was held in place by multiple clamps, and he worked as intently as a surgeon. Hannah didn't want to startle him and risk further damage to the mandolin, so she whispered his name as she knocked lightly on the doorjamb.

"I'll be with you in a minute, Hannah," Eddie responded as he continued applying a touch of glue and attached a tiny clamp to the neck of the mandolin. Once he was finished, he straightened and wiped his hands on a towel. "Do you have news?"

"I have a question." She saw his disappointment, so she hurried to add something hopeful. "I also have some updates on interviews I've done."

"Let's go sit outside to talk."

"Okay, but I'd rather ask my question in here first because I want to show you a photo. It will be easier to see without the glare of the sun." Hannah took out her phone and opened the screenshot. "I thought it might be too painful to watch the video, so I wanted to ask you just to look at this photo and tell me if you know who's playing the mandolin."

Hannah handed over her phone. She tried not to appear too obvious in watching Eddie study the photo, but it didn't matter. He was so transfixed by the image on her phone that she might have been miles away. A series of emotions flitted over his face, and when he raised his eyes to meet her gaze, she detected a glint of moisture in them.

"That's Ward's boy, Howard. We called him Junior to avoid confusion." Eddie's expression was distant. "He was a talented picker. Might have been better than me one day. May I ask why you want to know?"

Hannah felt a kick of something she couldn't quite call elation. Much as she was glad to have her belief confirmed by both Eddie and Beverly, she hated the suspicions it raised. She really didn't want Junior, who'd clearly been like a son to Eddie at one time, to be the person who'd stolen the mandolin and the money. It made no sense. He'd only been a child.

"Hannah?"

She shook off the question, knowing Eddie was waiting for her answer. "I met him two nights ago. When I saw this video, I thought it was him, but it was taken so long ago that I wasn't sure."

"Junior's playing at the festival? Monroe didn't tell me."

"She probably knew you'd be upset."

Eddie turned away without answering.

Hannah took a chance and spoke up. "He and some friends have been having jam sessions at my restaurant the last couple of nights. I'm sure they'd be thrilled if you joined them sometime."

When Eddie turned back, he had that faraway look in his eyes again. "Jam sessions are the best part of being a musician. Making music with friends who understand—it's indescribable." He coughed and changed the subject. "What were you going to tell me about the interviews?"

Hannah filled him in on the meeting with Maureen and about the visit she and Monroe had made to the storage company. "And just so you know, Sheriff Steele showed me the case files, and he agrees with you that Sheriff Crane dropped the ball. We'll keep working this until we have answers."

His voice was rough when he thanked her, so Hannah took that as her cue to move on. "I'll be in touch."

As she walked to her car, Hannah wished she had thought to ask him about the videos Monroe had mentioned, but when she glanced back, she saw him standing in the doorway, a solitary figure cradling his mandolin in his arms the way he must have held it to play so many years ago. Her heart ached for his pain, and she decided she'd leave the man in peace. Monroe could get the videos.

Blackberry Valley
June 1975

Eddie grabbed his fishing pole and headed down to the dock. Seemed like the lake was the only place he could find peace these days. If he heard one more argument about sound he might just have to agree with Ward and break up the band.

Eddie was so deep in his angry thoughts that he didn't even notice the boy sitting on the edge of the dock until he almost fell over him. "Junior, what are you doing here?"

Ward's nine-year-old son gave a shrug but didn't turn around.

"Are you looking for Sandy? She and Bev went into town. Some beauty parlor thing."

Junior still didn't look up, but he shook his head.

Eddie set his fishing pole down and lowered himself beside Junior with his legs swinging over the edge. That was when he noticed the banjo in the boy's lap. "You trying out a new instrument?"

"Pa says I have to learn it."

"Why?"

"'Cause you're the only mandolin player allowed round here."

Eddie's anger rose a notch. "I'll have a word with him."

Junior looked up then, and Eddie saw the misery on his face. "You mean it wasn't you who said I couldn't play no more?"

"Did your father say it was?"

Junior hung his head. "He said I could never measure up. I'd be better off learning the banjo like him."

It had been getting harder and harder to hold on to his temper when it seemed like the whole world was against him, but no way was Eddie going to let this poor kid bear the brunt of the grown-ups' battles.

"Did your pa ever teach you to fish?"

Junior shook his head. "He thinks it's a waste of time unless you're lookin' for dinner."

Eddie let out a belly laugh. "I'll let you in on a little secret. I toss back every fish I catch."

"Then why do you bother?"

"Because sitting out here alone brings me peace. I'll show you, and you let me know if you like it. Deal?"

At last, Junior cracked a grin. "Deal."

For the next hour, Eddie taught the boy the basics of fishing. When he finally had a good rhythm and was casting the line with a sure hand, Eddie decided it was time. "How do you like fishing?"

"Better than playing the banjo," Junior muttered.

Eddie let out a roar of laughter. "I'll tell you another secret, young man. You have exactly what it takes to be a first-rate mandolin player, and I'm going to teach you myself."

The boy's eyes glowed for a minute, but then fear shaded them. "But my pa—"

"Don't you worry about your pa. I'll talk with him and let him know I'll be honored to teach his boy. Now you run along up to the house. I just heard the car drive up, and I know Ms. Bev was going to stop at the bakery for treats."

Junior jumped up and threw his arms around Eddie. "Thank you, Mr. Eddie. You're the best."

Eddie sat alone for a long time after that, wondering how to talk to his friend. Some days it felt like there was nothing left of the friendship they'd started so long ago. And that nearly broke his heart.

Chapter Nineteen

By the time Hannah made it back to the Hot Spot, she was ready to set detective work aside for a bit and focus on food and friends. But even as she prepped food with Jacob and arranged place settings with Raquel and Dylan, she wondered if Junior and his friends would be back, or if she'd scared him off asking about playing the mandolin.

What should she do if he returned? Should she show him the video? Or should she wait for Monroe to get her grandfather's videos to see if they showed anything of interest? She didn't expect there to be film of someone walking away with the mandolin in hand. That would certainly have been reported to the sheriff, who would surely have done something about it. No, what she was hoping for was something more discreet, some clue that would point her in the right direction. Right now she felt like she was stumbling around in the dark, clueless.

Hannah and her team worked diligently to prep for the evening rush right up until she opened the door. Then they settled into their well-established routine. Hannah was talking to two of her regulars when the phone began to ring. Since Elaine was busy seating new arrivals, Hannah excused herself and made her way to the hostess stand. She grabbed the phone just as it stopped ringing. She answered anyway, hopeful that the caller was still on the line, waiting to leave a message. "Hello, are you there? This is the Hot Spot. May I help you?"

There was a quick intake of breath, and the line went dead. Hannah set the phone down and waited for a few minutes in case the person had been cut off and would call right back. When Elaine came over, Hannah told her what happened.

Elaine frowned. "That's the third time tonight, and there were several yesterday. Probably kids playing pranks."

"Speaking of pranks, Liam's had to deal with a number of fires out at the festival grounds," Hannah added. "He thinks they're either pranks or people being careless, but I wonder if someone is trying to sabotage the festival."

"What does Liam think about that?" Elaine asked.

"He said that the fires have had reasonable causes. I'm supposed to see him later, so I'll mention our hang-up calls. I don't think they're connected, but I'll see if he thinks we should be concerned." Then Hannah asked the question that had been weighing on her. "I don't see a reservation for the festival group tonight. Are they not coming?"

"They had to cancel. Apparently they have an evening sound check. It was supposed to be tomorrow night, but the forecast is calling for thunderstorms, so it seemed wiser to do it a day early."

Hannah couldn't question the wisdom of their decision, but she also couldn't help but wonder if her question to Junior had played into that choice. He'd seemed like the informal leader of their group, so if he'd wanted to avoid her, changing the tech schedule might have been convenient.

As Hannah walked back to the kitchen to see if Jacob could use a hand, she also did a mental reset. Surely she was taking herself too seriously to think an entire sound check would be rearranged because of her.

The rest of the night passed quickly, and Liam arrived shortly before closing. "No music tonight?" he asked Hannah when she greeted him.

"No. They had a sound check. I'm sorry to miss the music, but it's just as well that we close on time if you're going to help me go through the files Maureen Hughes loaned me."

"Detective Berthold on the case."

Hannah's mood lifted, as it always did when Liam was around. "Is my favorite detective hungry? I'll bet Jacob can rustle up something for you."

"I won't say no to that offer. I've been hearing rumors about his barbecue all day."

"Do you want to come into the kitchen or sit out here?"

Before Liam could answer, Jack Delaney walked through the door. "Am I pushing it coming this near to closing? I got caught up with a layout issue and lost track of time. I can scrounge up something at home if you're shutting down already."

"I just promised to serve Liam, so I'll hardly turn you away. Do you need a menu?"

"Not if Jacob's barbecue is still an option."

Hannah grinned. "When I tell him two hungry men came in late looking for his special, it might inflate his ego, but I guarantee the barbecue is worth it. I'll be back with the plates before you know it."

By the time Hannah came back with two hefty servings of barbecue and all the fixings, Jack and Liam were seated together, deep in conversation about baseball standings. No matter what the season, there was always some sports team that held their attention. Hannah meant to deliver the plates and leave them to their debate, but Jack called her back.

"Hannah, I've been meaning to message you. One part of your mystery is solved. I found the missing newspaper bins."

"Really? Where were they?"

"They were on the other side of the basement. Apparently there was a leak a few years before my time, and everything had to be moved away so the wall could be repaired." He made a face. "Seems these bins were overlooked when the shelves were reinstalled. That would also explain why those issues never got scanned. Nothing sinister after all. I have the back issues in my office if you want to read them. Does that take the reporter off your suspect list?"

"I guess so," Hannah admitted. "I'd already pretty much eliminated her. Lacy and I drove to Nashville this morning to talk with her, and she was quite open about everything. When I told her about the missing bins, she had her daughter dig out her old work files for me to go through."

"Good to hear. I didn't like thinking that someone in my profession, and attached to the *Chronicle* no less, could be involved in something so nefarious."

"I completely understand. Let me know if you two need anything else, all right?" Hannah headed back to the kitchen to begin cleanup. The sooner the restaurant was closed, the sooner she and Liam could get to work. She was pinning her hopes on there being some clue in the files. The festival opened in two days, and she didn't like the uncertainty of the theft hanging over it.

Once the Hot Spot was closed for the night, Hannah and Liam headed upstairs to go through the box of files Maureen had loaned her that morning.

Hannah was a bit surprised to see how meticulously everything was organized, but it made sense for someone who made their living from their writing. She and Jacob had the kitchen organized for ease and efficiency. It looked like Maureen had arranged her files the same way, making it easy for Hannah to differentiate between notes, drafts, and final submissions.

"This is like a step back in time," she remarked to Liam when they started to go through the folder labeled *Final Articles*. Some of the articles were handwritten in a neat and precise style, but others had clearly been typed on an old manual typewriter with carbon paper. "I'm so used to everything being computerized that it's strange to think of someone pecking away to write this. Imagine having to white-out every error or start over altogether."

"Someday someone will be wondering about us when they can write an article simply by thinking it into print," Liam teased.

"If we even need print. Maybe we'll just be able to look at each other to transfer thoughts."

"Like this?" Liam stared intently at Hannah, and she could almost see hearts glowing in his eyes.

"I love you too," she said, laughing. "Now, enough of the futuristic stuff. We have all this from the past. I think I want to read through her notebooks and see what she thought was important enough to record."

It wasn't long before Hannah realized that the answer to that was "everything." The beautiful penmanship of the finished articles was nowhere in sight in the notebooks. There were stains, and the writing was small and cramped, as if Maureen had been trying to cram as many details as she could into a small space.

As Hannah studied them, a pattern emerged from the notes. There were carefully recorded quotes from whoever was being interviewed down the left side of the page, but the right side was full of Maureen's personal thoughts, ideas, and follow-up questions.

After half an hour passed in silence disturbed only by the rustle of paper, Hannah looked over at Liam, who seemed to be struggling to stay awake while reading the *Chronicle* stories. "Have you found anything interesting yet?"

"I wish I could say yes and hand you a juicy clue, but everything I've read just reinforces what you've told me. She has articles previewing the festival. She must have come down early and hung around for rehearsals and visits with the performers." He leaned back and stretched. "I know you've mentioned feuding, but nothing I've read here gives even a hint of it. She writes positively about the Blackberry Mountain Boys and their music."

Hannah had to agree. "Everything I'm reading is the same. Maureen takes very detailed notes, but everything is effusive with praise for the musicians and festival."

When Liam yawned, she suggested they call it a night. "I had this unrealistic hope that we might find a smoking gun, but I don't think there's anything here that will solve the mystery. We'd both probably be better off getting some sleep instead."

Liam reluctantly agreed and kissed her good night. "Here's hoping you dream up the answer to the mystery."

Chapter Twenty

Hannah was up early Friday morning. Unfortunately, her dreams had provided no more answers than Maureen's files had. Wishing she were still asleep, she stumbled to the coffee maker and started it. Once it was ready, she tried to stifle a yawn as she began to pour hot coffee into her mug, but she accidentally spilled it down the side instead.

As the coffee hit her counter, a flash of understanding brought her fully awake. Maureen's notes had been covered with coffee stains—identical to the ones she'd noted on the police case files.

Hannah cleaned up the mess and filled her cup as she tried to wrap her brain around the implication. Last night, she'd been so frustrated by the lack of any obvious suspects in Maureen's files that she'd overlooked how closely the reporter's notes matched the sheriff's—down to the suggestion of an overeager fan making off with the mandolin, and the profits burning up in the fire. It made for a pretty wrap-up of a pointless investigation.

Was it possible that the mandolin part at least was correct? Hannah realized she was going to have to consider that possibility, as much as Eddie didn't want to believe it. Except, if a fan had taken the mandolin, how had it ended up back in storage? And what about the fact that Patrick said the fire department was certain that all the money had not been destroyed in the fire?

There was one other possibility that Hannah realized she hadn't considered, though it felt a little far-fetched. Whoever had stolen the mandolin could have had an attack of conscience and taken a job with the storage company when Beverly hired them, simply to return the mandolin.

Hannah shook her head and took another sip of her coffee. That sounded ridiculous even to her desperate self.

She started to gather up the files to replace them in the carton, and had almost finished when she remembered she'd left a folder down in the dining room the previous night. She'd been carrying it when she saw Liam out.

As soon as she opened her apartment door, she could hear the restaurant phone ringing. She jogged down the staircase. A reservation request, or another prank call? Hannah made a dash for the hostess stand and picked up. "Good morning. You've reached Blackberry Valley's Hot Spot. How may I help you?"

"Ms. Hannah Prentiss?"

"Speaking. What can I do for you, Junior?"

There was a moment's hesitation, and Hannah suspected that Junior had not expected her to recognize his voice.

"I was hoping we might speak privately. About what you asked me the other night."

Hannah wanted to say, *Yes, of course I want to talk to you and find out why you lied to me.* Instead she kept her voice neutral. "I'm here at the restaurant. I have to be at the library at eleven, but if you can come here before then, we can talk."

His reply was immediate. "I can be there in less than ten minutes."

"Okay. I'll unlock the front door, so come on in when you arrive."

Hannah briefly considered the wisdom of leaving the door open, but Junior was no threat to her. He just wanted to talk. This phone call did make her wonder whether he could have been the person making the other calls, but she immediately eliminated him as a suspect when she realized that he'd been in the midst of a jam session when at least one of the calls had occurred.

The calls bothered her more than they probably should. Both Elaine and Liam had shrugged them off as pranks, but Hannah couldn't shake the feeling that they were connected to the mandolin mystery. She had mentioned the calls to Liam the previous night and questioned whether they could be connected to the fires, but he still didn't think the fires out on the festival grounds were suspicious.

It was easier for Hannah to set aside her worries about them now that she had Junior's visit to speculate about. What did he have to tell her? She tried to wrestle her expectations into submission as she headed back upstairs with the folder and quickly finished packing the boxes before Junior arrived. It wasn't as if he was coming to reveal who had stolen Eddie's mandolin. He merely wanted to explain his lie—didn't he?

Since her coffee had gone cold, Hannah decided to put on a pot in the kitchen before she went to unlock the door. When she reached the front, she found Junior already waiting. He looked distinctly uncomfortable, a far cry from the self-assured musician who had jammed with his friends earlier in the week.

Hannah greeted him and invited him into the dining room. "I just put on a fresh pot of coffee. Would you like some?"

He seemed ready to decline, then changed his mind. "If it's no trouble."

She smiled warmly and waved at him to follow her into the kitchen. "No trouble at all. I had a late night, so I'm in need of caffeine myself."

"I hope I didn't wake you."

"No. We missed the music last night. How did sound check go?"

"Went off without a hitch." Junior seemed grateful for the casual conversation while they waited on the coffee, settling on stools at the kitchen counter. He told her about the lineup of acts and how enthusiastic everyone was. "Everything should be ready for the festival to begin on schedule."

"That's great news."

An idea had popped into Hannah's head as they chatted. It seemed better to bring it up now before she mentioned the videos, in case he wasn't feeling as cooperative afterward. "I'm wondering if you can help me with something, Junior. Eddie's granddaughter, Monroe, asked me to help investigate what happened at the festival in '76. I would really like to speak with your father about it, but I'm not sure how to get in touch with him."

"Why do you need to talk to Dad?"

Hannah ignored his wary tone and replied in a friendly voice. "He was Eddie's good friend up until that night. He might have some insight or could have seen something that he wasn't even aware of. Sheriff Steele always advises people just to tell us everything they can think of, and we'll decide if it's important."

Junior swallowed so hard that he started to cough, and Hannah noticed he had gone a shade paler.

"You work with the sheriff?"

She had to be honest. "Not officially, but I have helped solve a number of cases over the past year, so we often work together like we're doing on this case."

"I doubt my dad would know anything that he didn't tell the sheriff back then."

Hannah gave him a smile. "We've discovered that Sheriff Crane—that was his name—didn't really put much effort into figuring out who took the mandolin. We're trying harder now because Eddie needs to know. So how can I talk to your father?"

Junior let out a sigh. "My dad likes to video chat with me when we're on the road. I could call him and let you talk, but please don't question him too hard. That was a rough time in his life."

"I'm sure it was. He bounced back nicely with his new band though."

Junior shook his head sadly. "Not really. It was never the same. He and Eddie were something special together, something he could never replicate."

Hannah felt his sorrow, but she had hope. "If I can solve this, maybe we can get your father and Eddie to perform together at the festival. It might be good for both of them."

Junior's expression brightened. "I like the way you think, Hannah. Even if it is a pipe dream."

She shrugged. "We'll never know unless we try, right? So let's start with the video call."

Junior's smile faded, but he took out his phone and made the call.

His father picked up on the third ring. "Junior, my boy. It's good to see you. How's everything going with the festival?"

Hannah stayed out of sight to give Junior a chance to speak with his father first, but she could hear everything clearly.

Junior smiled. "It's been great, Dad. We've had some weather issues, but the rehearsals have been smooth, and we've been having terrific jam sessions at a restaurant here in the valley."

"Great. Jam sessions were always my favorite part. Hanging out with friends. Making music together."

"Speaking of them, I've got the owner of the restaurant here. She wanted to say hello to you and ask you a few questions."

Junior handed his phone to Hannah, who got her first chance to see what Ward looked like today. The full mane of hair she'd seen in the videos was silver now, but his eyes twinkled with the same lively spirit.

"Hello, Mr. Burton. My name's Hannah. I own the Hot Spot here in Blackberry Valley, and I'm the lucky one who's gotten to host these jam sessions."

"Please, call me Ward. All my friends do, and anyone who would host jam sessions for my son and his band is a friend of mine."

"That's very kind. I asked Junior if I could speak with you. I assume you've heard that Eddie Conley's missing mandolin was found."

"I've heard. Kinda strange after all these years, and pretty coincidental that it appeared just as the festival was starting. I imagine that will increase revenue."

Hannah felt her eyes widen. "I hadn't thought of it that way, but it's an interesting point. Junior didn't mention this, but I'm helping our Sheriff Steele investigate what happened. I was wondering if there is anything you remember that might point us in the right direction."

Ward's face deepened into a scowl. "I didn't take the mandolin, young lady, if that's what you're suggesting."

"Oh, not at all," Hannah hastened to assure him. "I've spoken with Eddie about that, and he feels absolutely awful that he accused you. The sheriff knows you had nothing to do with the disappearance."

Ward's relief was visible. "Well, that's good. As for anything else, I told the old sheriff everything I could remember. I was livid after that accusation, so I can't say I was thinking clearly enough to have noticed anything out of the ordinary. Did you speak to my son about it? He was just a young'un but since he wasn't involved, he might have seen something that makes more sense now than it did then."

Hannah felt Junior stiffen beside her. He reached for the phone. Hannah didn't want to hand it over, but she also realized there wasn't anything more she was likely to get from Ward. "I'll do that. It's been nice talking to you, Ward. I hope you'll consider coming to Blackberry Valley for the festival. We'd love to have you."

"Thank you for the offer, Hannah. Goodbye."

She handed over the phone, but not before she noticed a wistful expression cross Ward's face. He'd neither agreed nor refused to come, and she could only hope that she'd planted a seed of an idea that would take root.

Junior shared a few more moments of conversation with his father, and Hannah considered Ward's suggestion that she speak to Junior about what he remembered. Again the question rose in her mind—why had he lied about playing the mandolin? It was time for some answers, but she needed to tread carefully so as not to drive him away before she got them.

When Junior disconnected his call, Hannah said, "I hope your dad will decide to come to the festival. I'm really looking forward to it, especially since I watched videos of some of the original festivals. It looked like a fun time."

Junior didn't seem to agree. His face had taken on an unhealthy tinge, and he looked ill at ease. The suspicions that had been nudging her gathered force.

The coffee had finished brewing, so she poured him a cup and offered him cream and sugar.

He barely noticed. "You saw me in the videos, didn't you? That's why you asked about the mandolin."

"I did. I wasn't trying to trick you or anything when I asked. I was genuinely curious. I didn't get suspicious until you denied playing."

Junior swallowed hard and closed his eyes as he leaned against the counter. For a moment, Hannah thought she might have to call for medical help. But at last he opened his eyes, and she could see what almost looked like peace.

"Do you want to drink your coffee before you tell me what happened to the mandolin?" she asked quietly.

He shook his head. "I want to get this over with. You've obviously figured it out. Yes, I used to play the mandolin. My dad wasn't happy about it because that was Eddie's instrument, but Eddie was like a second dad to me. He taught me everything he knew."

"He said you would have been better than him one day."

Panic crossed Junior's face. "You talked to him?"

"I asked him to verify that it was you in the video. He said you were a fine picker, one of the best."

"He wouldn't have been so generous if he knew what I did."

Hannah deliberately gentled her voice. "What *did* you do, Junior?"

"I borrowed his mandolin, and I broke it."

Hannah waited to see if he had anything else to say, but those words seemed to have depleted him. "You couldn't have been more than nine or ten in that video."

He nodded. "Ten. That's the age Dad and Eddie said I had to be to play onstage. That was my first and last Blackberry Valley festival until this week." Junior placed his elbows on the counter and buried his face in his hands.

Hannah reached across to him. "Junior, you were just a boy. Whatever you did is long in the past."

He inhaled and then let out a long, heartfelt sigh. "That one event has been with me every day of my life. You have to understand. I adored Eddie Conley. He was everything I wanted to be when I grew up. I know my dad was a talented musician too, but Eddie had a kind of mystique about him."

"From what Eddie told me, he was extremely fond of you as well."

Junior nodded and cleared his throat. "I so wanted to be like him that during the dinner hour, when Dad and Eddie were in the trailer arguing over their future, I borrowed his mandolin and went out on the stage and played it."

Hannah held her breath.

"I was just playing for myself. I'd always watched Eddie picking that mandolin and wondered what was so special about it that he sounded so good. I was lost in the music, totally caught up in the moment, playing my heart out, but then all of a sudden I heard the crew coming to get ready for the next set." He swallowed hard. "I panicked. I was afraid that someone would see me, so I hurried off the stage. Then I heard my dad's voice. That's when I fell."

Hannah could see his hands trembling.

"I will never forget the sound of that bridge snapping."

She let the words hang for a few minutes as he recovered himself. Finally she asked, "What did you do?"

"I ran away. I threw the mandolin into an open box and shoved it behind some crates. Then I beat it back to the trailer and hid in my bedroom. I pretended to be asleep when I heard the shouting about the mandolin being gone."

"Why did you take the money?"

Junior's head shot up, and he gaped at her in shock. "I didn't take the money. I promise I had nothing to do with that."

Hannah believed him. After telling the truth about the mandolin, there was no reason for him to lie about the money.

"This might sound like a dumb question from someone who isn't a musician, but would anyone in the audience have been able to tell it was Eddie's mandolin you were playing, rather than your own?" Hannah was wondering why no one in the audience had spoken up to point a finger at Junior.

"No. From that distance, the instruments would all look pretty much the same. And they'd seen me picking my own mandolin in the set right before the break. Probably no one would have thought a kid would be bold enough to touch Eddie's precious mandolin. I wouldn't have normally, but we'd been playing together all afternoon, and I was so in awe of him. I wanted to see if some of that instrument's magic would rub off on me."

"The mandolin that Monroe and I found had been glued back together." Hannah thought of the sloppy work that suddenly made sense. "Did you do that?"

Junior nodded miserably.

"Why didn't you just say something to your dad? Surely he or Eddie would have understood."

Junior took a gulp of coffee, clearly trying to steady his nerves. "I knew Eddie's mandolin was off-limits. He allowed no one to touch it, much less play it. It was a gift from Bill Monroe, and Eddie cared for it as if it were a newborn baby. It was the instrument he made his magical music on. And I destroyed it."

Hannah wanted to argue with his thinking, but she didn't because she had seen how possessive Eddie was of that mandolin. She could only imagine what it had seemed like to a child who revered him.

Junior looked at Hannah with red-rimmed eyes, and she could see the scared young boy he had been in every line on his face. "I know I should have gone out and fessed up. I started to, honestly. But when I got outside, Eddie was yelling at my dad, accusing him of stealing the mandolin to break them up." He slowly shook his head as if to get rid of the memory. "If I close my eyes, I can still see it more vividly than any video could have captured. A crowd had gathered around them, and Eddie had a look I'd never seen before. As an adult, I understand that it was rage fueled by his heartbreak, but as a kid I was petrified of that anger being turned against me."

Hannah wanted to cry for the scared boy, but her heart also ached for Eddie, who'd spent fifty years stuck in a time warp because of a child's mistake and his own temper. "So when did you fix the mandolin?"

"The final evening session was about to begin. Dad and Eddie called a temporary truce so they could finish the festival and not disappoint the fans, but the tension in the air felt like a storm was about to break. I guess you could say that happened in the second set. Eddie was using a backup instrument and couldn't hit his stride. He muddled through at first, but then he got angry all over again."

Hannah could imagine how that had gone.

"At first I thought they were putting on a performance for the crowd, but it didn't take long to see that Eddie was genuinely accusing my father of having something to do with his missing mandolin. The shouting was terrifying. I don't know what happened next because I beat it out of there as soon as I heard Eddie start blaming my father again."

All of this matched what Hannah had read and heard about the account, even down to the onstage breakup of the band.

"I was so scared someone would find it and somehow know it was me who'd broken it, so I pretended I was cleaning up and checking the boxes, then I carried some back to our trailer. While everyone else was fighting, I grabbed some glue and fixed it as well as I could. I was only ten of course, so I lacked the necessary skills to do the repair correctly. I snuck back to the stage and put the box with all the other instruments. I figured someone would find it when they were cleaning up and give it back to Eddie."

Obviously, that hadn't happened.

He gave a wry grimace. "Not exactly the clearest thinking, but it was the best I could come up with. When I heard that the money had gone missing too, but no one had found the mandolin, I convinced myself that whoever had taken the money had also discovered the mandolin and kept it. So what good would it do for me to confess? It didn't exactly absolve me of responsibility, but to my ten-year-old conscience it made sense."

Hannah understood why he might have reasoned that way.

Junior slumped down over the counter. "I guess I need to go see Eddie and confess—fifty years too late."

"You definitely should, but maybe not yet."

The shock on Junior's face was mixed with relief. "Why not?"

"Because I believe you," Hannah replied. "But if you had nothing to do with the stolen money, then I need to figure out who did. If you confess, they might blame you for that too, and the real thief will get away with it altogether."

"You don't trust Eddie to keep quiet?"

Hannah took her time answering. She tried to think of all the angles while she sipped her coffee. "I think we can't be sure how he will react. It's bound to be a shock." She took another sip before posing a question. "Do you think your father suspects you were involved?"

Junior shook his head. "Absolutely not. He would have dragged me to confess to Eddie regardless of the outcome." He hung his head. "He's going to be so ashamed of me."

She didn't know Ward well enough to judge how he might react, but she hoped he would remember that Junior had been a child and be kind to him—even though his actions had been the final straw that had broken up a years-long friendship.

"You'll have to tell him too, you know."

Junior nodded miserably.

"I have an idea."

He met her gaze, something like hope flickering in his eyes.

"When I was talking with your father, I could see from his expression that he is really torn about coming to the festival. I think you should go get him. Convince him to come. And then when he is here, you can explain everything to your father and Eddie at the same time. That will also give me a little longer to try to figure out who took the money."

Junior didn't look entirely convinced, but some of the tension eased from his body.

"How long would it take you to get him and come back?"

He shrugged. "A couple of hours. He lives outside Louisville."

"Does he still play banjo?"

Junior smiled for the first time since he'd begun his confession. "And sings like a bird."

Hannah sighed. "My dream was to have both Ward and Eddie reunited before the festival. I've still got twenty-four hours, so I'm not giving up yet."

He appraised her. "If you can somehow do that, it would be a miracle."

"Will you go get your dad?"

Junior bowed his head, but this time it was more in reverence than defeat, and Hannah suspected he was praying. When he lifted his head, his expression was clear. "I will."

Hannah had an urge to hug him, but she settled for a warm smile. "Thank you. I'll do the best I can to uphold my end of this deal. Right now, I have to head over to the library to help finalize the presentation and pick up some items to display here for the festival, but I'll be in touch."

Hannah took the coffee cups to the sink and washed her hands, then faced Junior once more. "I want you to know how much I appreciate the trust you put in me by sharing your story. It is safe with me until you can share it with your father and Eddie. I hope that with the wisdom of age, they will understand that a frightened boy never meant to cause such a fallout."

Junior took her hands in his, clasping them like they were a lifeline. "Thank you for listening. Telling someone after all these years has lifted a great burden that I've carried alone. In my head, I know I was a scared boy who made a mistake. I have spent every day of my life since, atoning for that mistake. But that can't recapture what was lost to them. The mandolin, yes, but the friendship even more."

"Monroe also said the loss of their friendship was what hurt Eddie most. You need to remember that from all reports, they were well on their way to breaking up before this happened. Besides, yes, you were a child, but they were grown men who had differences and should have been able to resolve them without instigating a feud."

Junior laughed. "That sounds like something my mother would have said. She was a wise woman."

Hannah smiled at him and squeezed his hands. "I'll take that as a compliment. Now, I need to get going. Evangeline is waiting for me. Would you like to come visit the library and see the exhibit?"

"I should have time for that, though I'm due for a rehearsal in an hour."

"Good. Maybe you can tell us if we're missing anything important."

Chapter Twenty-One

Hannah and Junior strolled along the street in the warm June sun. "I understand we might be in for some storms overnight," she said. "I hope they don't flood the festival grounds."

"That's why we did sound check last night. A little mud in the field won't stop the show, but if there's lightning we'll have to cut power and clear the area. So here's hoping the storms move through overnight."

As they climbed the steps to the library, Hannah explained about the exhibit and how they'd hoped to showcase the history of the festival years while educating visitors about bluegrass music.

"And this is where you found the mandolin?"

"Yes. The bulk of the display came from the crates Beverly Conley loaned to the library."

Junior shook his head. "I wonder how long it would have stayed hidden if Harry White hadn't decided to revive the festival."

When they entered the library, Hannah was thrilled to discover that order had been restored. She felt guilty that she hadn't been back to help. Evangeline reassured her that there were plenty of volunteers, but only one Hannah who could solve the mystery.

With the start of the festival looming, those words weighed on Hannah like a ticking clock. She tried to shove them aside because it would take a clear head to figure out the final pieces. To her mind, the most important part of the mystery had been solved. Eddie would know why his mandolin had been broken and hidden. How he took the news remained to be seen, but Hannah had to trust in God that Eddie would have the wisdom to see the part his anger had played.

Evangeline waved, and Hannah greeted her, then introduced Junior.

"Goodness, it's such an honor to meet you," Evangeline gushed. "We're all so excited for the festival and to hear you play."

Hannah smiled at Junior, hoping that such praise would be a balm to his injured soul. "You're in for a treat," she promised the librarian. "I've been fortunate to see a preview at the Hot Spot. All of the players are amazing."

"Pleasure to meet you, Evangeline. Do you have a favorite bluegrass song? We'd be happy to play it for you as a thank-you for all the work you've done to support our festival."

Evangeline thought for a moment. "Do you think you could play 'I'm Working on the Road to Glory Land'? My husband and I saw Flatt and Scruggs in concert once, and we loved that song. It will thrill him if you play that."

Junior promised, then wandered away to take in the various elements of the display.

"You pulled it all together. The exhibit looks fantastic," Hannah told Evangline.

"I had a lot of help," Evangeline replied. "And, of course, most of the credit goes to Phyllis and Beverly. Without Phyllis's eye for detail and Beverly's supplying all of this, we would have had nothing. Oh, I have something new to show you. Monroe told me she was trying to get some old videos for you to watch."

Hannah grimaced. "I was really hoping they would hold some clues, but Monroe left me a message last night that the film has degraded too much. She said she was going to send them off to see if they could be restored, but it will take a while to see if it works. I was really hoping to solve this before the festival."

"Maybe what I have will help. When Beverly was looking for those videos, she found a whole box of festival photos. She dropped them off last night, so I only had time for a quick glance. I can tell you that they're not in any order and aren't in the best shape. Some are pretty faded. I was hoping to find a way to display them without the light doing any damage, but I haven't had a chance this morning. They're in my office if you want to see them."

Hope lifted Hannah's spirits. "That would be wonderful. Let me go say goodbye to Junior. He has to leave for a rehearsal soon anyway."

Junior was standing in front of a table that displayed memorabilia from the festival, programs and photos from every year of its too-short run. "That one was before I was even born," he told Hannah when she joined him. "I grew up on the stories Dad and Eddie told about how it turned from a dream they talked about into something that exceeded their wildest expectations."

Hannah felt sadness emanating from him. "When I figure this out, we'll give them a chance to have it all back again. Just think how exciting that will be."

Junior smiled at her. "You make this old man's heart feel young and hopeful again."

Hannah snorted at his description of himself. "Evangeline has some photos for me to go through, so I came to say goodbye." She glanced around, but since there was no one within hearing distance, she continued. "I'm going to do everything I can to solve the rest of this, but I will make you a promise. If I can't figure it out before tomorrow, we'll still go talk to Eddie, so he and your dad can hopefully reunite for the festival. Deal?"

Junior gave a short nod. "Deal."

She returned to Evangeline, who had the box of photos waiting.

"I have to go do story hour," the librarian explained, "but why don't you take these to a table so you can spread out?"

Hannah would have preferred something more private, but other than the families waiting on story time, the library was all but empty. This early on a Friday morning, most people were at work. School had already let out for the summer, so most kids were at home or camp. She basically had the reading room to herself.

Just as Hannah set the box on a table, she heard fire truck sirens, so she paused to say a prayer for the safety of whoever needed help and the emergency personnel who would provide it. "Be safe, Liam," she whispered at the end of the prayer.

The truck had been headed out of town in the direction of the festival grounds. Hannah hoped there wasn't more trouble there. Knowing that Liam would handle whatever had happened, Hannah turned her attention to the box of photos. She pulled out a chair, sat at the table and lifted the lid on the box.

Her hopes immediately plummeted. Evangeline hadn't been kidding. The box was chaos—hundreds of photos tossed in haphazardly. Hannah lifted one from the top and flipped it over. Thank goodness there was a date. Rather than waste time checking all of the photos, she removed a handful and examined the backs. Not every photo had a date, but most did, so she was able to sort those by year. That would be helpful for Evangeline's display, but it also allowed her not to waste time studying past years when she needed to focus on 1976.

When she had a small pile with the pertinent dates, she spread them out on the table. Since these were the most recent, the images were clearer than some of the ones from the previous decade. The first thing she noticed was the proliferation of American flags. That made sense, since it was the bicentennial year. Those flags would also help her identify any relevant photos from the undated pile.

Hannah picked up one photo that showed the stage. The photo was taken from a distance, so she took out her phone and opened the magnifier app. When she zoomed in on the stage, she could see Ward and Eddie in the center. She recognized some of the other players from conversations with Beverly and Monroe. Huck played guitar, Melvin was on Dobro, and Jasper was their bass player. Hannah wondered what had become of them. Had they joined Ward's new band—the one he formed so soon after the Blackberry Mountain Boys' breakup?

Hannah stopped her wandering thoughts. She knew what had happened to the mandolin, so what she really needed to look for was any photo that might show the ticket booth.

She laid the photos in a row and ran her magnifier over them. Nothing suspicious, but there was a man in uniform. He must be Sheriff Crane. And the woman beside him who gazed at him in adoration matched an author photo Hannah had seen recently.

Hannah thought about the matching stains on the police files and Maureen's notepad, and wondered again about the connection she'd made that morning. Had the relationship been real, or had Maureen been flirting with the sheriff in order to get access to the files? As intriguing as the question was, Hannah shrugged it off. She had more important information to look for than evidence of the sheriff's flirtation with a reporter.

It wasn't long before another photo caught her eye. One of the people in the snapshot was a much younger Beverly Conley. But who was the man she was talking to? And if this was Beverly, then she hadn't taken the photo. Who had?

A glance through the rest of the photos didn't turn up any others of Beverly or the mysterious man, so Hannah grabbed the one of Beverly. She left a note for Evangeline that she was borrowing one of the photos and set the box back on the circulation desk before heading back to the Hot Spot to get her car.

Beverly had been anxious about something related to this festival since the mandolin had surfaced. Or had she become concerned earlier, but Hannah hadn't noticed? Did her anxiety have anything to do with the man in this photo? But if it did, why had Beverly given it to Evangeline? Had she forgotten about the photo, or not known it was in the box?

Or did she finally want to come clean, just like Junior had?

Chapter Twenty-Two

Monroe answered the door when Hannah arrived at Eddie's house. "Hannah, what a surprise! Please tell me you're here to say that you solved the mystery."

More than anything, Hannah wished she could do that, but if she had made Junior wait to confess, she couldn't be the one to betray his secret. "Not the whole thing, but I think I'm getting close."

"That's good news. I'm sorry I can't stay to visit right now, but my mom and I were just heading to rehearsal."

"That's okay. I just wanted to ask Beverly about the photos she loaned to the library. But I hope I can at least say hello to your mother. I can't believe she's been back in town a couple of days and I haven't even seen her yet. The bands have been coming to jam at the Hot Spot almost every night. You should join us."

Monroe glanced around before whispering. "I've wanted to, but Nana has been even more on edge, so Mom didn't want to leave her alone." Her voice rose, and her tone grew brighter. "Here she comes. Mom, come say hello to Hannah."

Sandy Taylor was as lovely as Hannah remembered, and in person she could feel the warmth that was missing in all the tabloid photos. Sandy hurried over and wrapped Hannah in a bear hug. "Hannah, how good it is to see you." She lowered her voice to a whisper. "Thank you so much for all you're doing to help my parents."

She pulled back and grasped Hannah's hands. "I hear you've been holding jam sessions at your restaurant. Monroe and I are going to try to make it tonight."

"I hope you do. It's been an unexpected bonus of the festival. Junior is such a sweet man, though I admit I'm still struggling to call a sixty-year-old man Junior."

Sandy gave the trademark husky laugh Hannah remembered so well. "I've run into him a few times at other venues, but it's nice to be able to spend time getting to know him now."

Hannah couldn't help but wonder if she'd still feel that way once the truth came out, but she sincerely hoped everyone would understand and forgive a child's mistake.

"I know you and Monroe have to hurry off, but I was hoping to speak with your mother for a few minutes about some photos she loaned to Evangeline. If you think she's up to a visitor."

"She's actually expecting another visitor soon, but I'm sure she'll have time for you. This way."

Sandy led Hannah back to the porch where Beverly sat reading. "Look, Mama. You have a visitor before your visitor." She winked at Hannah before leaving.

Beverly twisted in her chair. Her face filled with anxiety when she saw Hannah, but her manners remained hospitable. "Good morning, Hannah. I wish Sandy had offered you some refreshment before she dashed off."

"That's all right," Hannah assured her as she took a seat across from Beverly. "I won't stay long. I just wanted to ask for your help with something." Hannah withdrew the photo from her purse. "Evangeline Cooke showed me the box of photos you delivered to her. I sorted through them to look at the ones from the final festival. There was a picture with someone in it that I didn't recognize. I was hoping you could identify him for me."

Beverly's face relaxed a fraction at the request. "Of course, dear, but I may need my glasses. Could I trouble you to get them from the table in the parlor?"

Hannah thought about leaving the photo with her, but since she wanted to see Beverly's face when she looked at it, she held onto it as she went into the house. She returned quickly and handed the glasses to Beverly, then sat across from her and held out the photo.

Beverly straightened her glasses as she took it. Her hands started to tremble, and her face grew pale. After a moment, she set the photo in her lap. "I'm sorry, dear. It's too blurry for me to be sure."

Hannah couldn't be disrespectful and call Beverly's bluff, but she did stare at the woman's trembling hands as she spoke. "Not a problem. I have a magnifier on my phone. The image is quite clear when I use that. Here, let me show you." Hannah moved to kneel beside Beverly's chair.

Beverly had closed her eyes, so Hannah wrapped her hands around the fragile ones that held the photo. "It's okay, Beverly. Whoever he is, you can tell me in complete confidence."

Beverly opened her eyes, and they were filled with a mix of grief and fear as she gave just a hint of a nod. "Eddie must never know, but I need to say it, because with all the stories about the festivals circulating and the mandolin being found—well, keeping the secret is killing me."

Hannah moved to sit on the edge of the table in front of Beverly, but she kept hold of the older woman's hands. Today seemed to be her day to be chosen as confidante. After her earlier conversation with Junior, she was almost afraid to hear what Beverly was going to say.

When Beverly licked her dry lips, Hannah handed her a glass of water from the side table. "Take your time. There's no rush."

Beverly took a sip of water and handed Hannah the glass. "I have loved Eddie Conley with my whole entire heart since he pulled my pigtails in second grade so he could show me his pet frog. The day he asked me to marry him was the best day of my life, second only to our wedding day."

She paused for another sip of water, and Hannah had a moment to think how much she understood what Beverly was saying. The day Liam proposed to her would live with her forever.

Beverly lowered her head a moment before she started to speak again. "But loving someone, being married to them, is not always easy. Every marriage has rocky spots, of course, but when your husband's job takes him on the road all the time, away from home and family—well, sometimes it all seems like too much." She picked up the photo. "This man was a friend." She paused and sighed. "And my pastor. I was talking to him about the struggles I was having in my marriage. That's where I was when the mandolin disappeared. At his office, asking for guidance." She closed her eyes and breathed softly. "I knew how important Eddie's music was to him, and touring was a huge part of that, but I was drowning. Eddie was my whole life, but I wasn't his. That was breaking me. I didn't know what to do."

She opened her eyes and took a deep breath. "But then the mandolin was stolen. Eddie was desperate, and he turned to me. I know it sounds pathetic to say that out loud, but it wasn't how it felt. It was as if it took the loss of his music to remind him that he had a wife who loved him. Not at first, of course. He carried an unfathomable sadness in those first few weeks, but after it became clear the sheriff would have no answers, something changed. We started over and rebuilt our marriage and our family. Eddie had always loved Sandy, but with the music gone, he became a doting father. Eventually he began to share his music with her, and that helped him too." She hung her head. "I have always felt guilty because Eddie lost so much when that mandolin was stolen, but I got my life back."

"You've never told Eddie this?"

"No, and I don't want him to ever know how lost I felt in our marriage back then. It wouldn't serve any productive purpose, and it would hurt him deeply. And that's why I've been so nervous. The possibility of this coming out has kept me up at night. I'm so afraid that it would ruin what we have now."

Hannah had witnessed how this had tortured Beverly, and it certainly made sense of her behavior. "I promise not to tell him, but maybe you should consider doing so, to ease the burden it has been on you."

Beverly shook her head sadly. "I can't risk it. Telling him now would just reopen old wounds for no reason."

Hannah wanted to argue, but what did she know about marriage? Beverly and Eddie had been married for over fifty years, and she'd been engaged for less than two months. "I know this has been a terrible strain. Thank you for trusting me and for explaining the photo. Do you want me to leave it with you so no one sees it at the museum?"

"Please shred it."

She had to choke back a laugh at the vehemence in the elderly lady's voice. "I will. Now would you look at another photo and give me your impression?" Hannah showed her the photo of Maureen and Sheriff Crane. She was not expecting the reaction she got.

Beverly rolled her eyes. "Bless her heart. She flirted shamelessly with the sheriff just to get her story. I guess it worked for her in the end. I think she was the one other person who benefited from Eddie's mandolin disappearing. Her stories on it drew national attention and gave her a whole different life. I was happy for her because her family members were awful. They feuded with Eddie and Ward out of sheer jealousy and tried one too many times to stop the festival. But in the end, she got her new life. Even wrote a book."

"I met her the other day. Lacy and I went up to Tennessee to talk to Maureen in the hope she might have some idea of what happened."

"Did she?"

"Unfortunately, no. But she did loan me all her research files from back then to go through. Liam and I spent time doing that last night."

Beverly clicked her tongue. "That is no way for an engaged couple to spend an evening. I'm sorry your romance time was taken up with our problems."

Hannah laughed. "We had fun. Surely you know by now that just being together is more than enough."

Beverly's face glowed with a benevolent smile. "With that attitude, I predict a long and happy life for the two of you."

"Thank you. I'll see myself out so I don't get in the way of your next visitor." Her spirits were light from Beverly's parting words as she headed to the front door. She opened it and almost walked right into a woman. "Hello, Shelby. Remember me? I'm Hannah Prentiss."

For a moment, Shelby had a deer-in-the-headlights look that puzzled Hannah.

"We met the other night at my restaurant," Hannah reminded her.

Shelby regained her composure and returned the greeting. "I'm sorry. It was disorienting to see you in a different setting. Beverly didn't tell me she had other company."

"I surprised her. She's out on the porch. Do you know the way?"

"Quite well. Beverly and I have been friends for decades."

Hannah smacked her forehead. "Of course you have been. Your husband managed the Blackberry Mountain Boys, didn't he?"

"He did, and he went on to manage Ward's band after the boys broke up."

"How lovely that you were still able to remain friends with Beverly despite your husbands disagreeing over the band's future."

"It was hard at first, but we deeply valued our friendship and had no use for foolishness that should have been worked through."

As Hannah walked to her car, she reflected that those may have been the wisest words she'd heard all week.

Since she'd gotten such an early start, Hannah decided to stop by Blackberry Market and pick up lunch to surprise Liam and whoever else was on duty. She was the one who was surprised when she got to the firehouse, only to find that the entire crew was still out on the call she'd heard at the library that morning. She went back to the kitchen and stored the food in the refrigerator.

She was heading back down the hallway when she noticed that Smoky, the firehouse dog, had followed her. She glanced down at the poor fellow, who looked as forlorn as she felt. "Don't like being left here alone, do you?"

Hannah sat down against the wall outside Liam's office and beckoned Smoky over. "Come sit with me. I'll keep you company for a while."

Once she was settled on the floor with the dog pressed against her leg, Hannah dug in her bag and pulled out her notebook. Maybe the change of scenery would help her gain some insight while she reviewed her notes.

She started by writing down what she knew. First was the solution to the missing mandolin. She didn't write that out because she didn't want to risk anyone seeing Junior's name, so she just put a small check mark beside that. She moved down to the mystery about the festival profits, marking that with a large *2*. She ran a hand through Smoky's fur as she mulled over potential suspects.

Beverly Conley had been the initial suspect in both mysteries, as she'd told Hannah and Monroe, but she'd had an alibi that checked out. So who else was there to consider?

According to the notes from the police files and Maureen's box of records, there had been five other main suspects—if she could even call them that, since Sheriff Crane hadn't done much to investigate them. At the top of that list had been Martin Lowe, the Blackberry Mountain Boys' manager and Shelby's deceased husband. He wasn't alive to interview, but she could talk to Shelby. Too bad she hadn't thought of that when they'd run into each other out at the Conley house earlier. Maybe Shelby would come in for dinner tonight. If not, Hannah could drop by the B&B and leave a message for her to get in touch. If nothing else, Shelby might have some ideas regarding other suspects.

Hannah wasn't completely without clues to ponder when it came to Martin. According to Maureen's files, he had topped the suspect list because of the feud between Eddie and Ward. Martin knew that if they broke up he'd be out of a job, so maybe he'd hoped that a mystery might keep them together. According to Maureen's scribbled comment, the waning popularity of bluegrass festivals at the time made it unlikely he would find another situation as successful as managing the Blackberry Mountain Boys.

Hannah scratched behind Smoky's ear, and the dog gave a satisfied groan. "What do you think, Smoky? Wouldn't he have been better off trying to keep them together?" She sighed. Stealing the mandolin of his breadwinner made absolutely no sense. Hannah tapped the pen against her notebook as she thought. Knowing who'd taken the mandolin changed things. Martin stealing the money did make sense for financial reasons—perhaps he wanted to tide himself over until his next gig—so he would remain on the list, at least until she talked with Shelby.

The other person with similar financial interests was the promoter, Arthur White. He was also deceased. Hannah checked her notes. The sheriff had eliminated him as a suspect at the time because he handled all the money anyway and would be paid for running the festival whether the band broke up or not. Of course, he did stand to lose if future festivals were canceled, but according to the case notes, he promoted plenty of other festivals, many with better-known headliners, so he was less likely to be concerned about losing this one.

Hannah fished her phone out of her pocket and did a quick internet search. Arthur White had died a wealthy man, and the sheer number of festivals and concerts listed under his name made her think Blackberry Valley's festival proceeds would be like a single raindrop falling on Noah's ark. Negligible impact in the grand scheme of things. She could talk to his wife and son, but would the son have brought the festival back here if they suspected Arthur's involvement? Arthur White could safely drop to the bottom rung of her list.

With that notation made, Hannah moved on to the next suspect, Ward Burton himself. She'd enjoyed talking with him earlier, but unfortunately that didn't eliminate him as a suspect regarding the money. Hannah knew that originally he'd been implicated only because of Eddie's ranting, but even Eddie had admitted that there was no basis for the blame. Besides, it had actually been his son who had taken the mandolin.

But what about the financial considerations for Ward? Hannah frowned, trying to remember exactly what Monroe had said to Colin about him. She made a note to tell Colin about her conversation with Ward, which reminded her that she needed to check in with the sheriff to see if he'd made any progress on his part of the investigation. She owed it to him to tell him about Junior's confession too, though she really wished she could wait until she had a more viable suspect for the theft of the money. She did have an obligation to report it, though, so she would call as soon as she got home.

Back to Monroe's comments. Hannah chewed on her bottom lip as she wrote what she recalled. Ward had expensive tastes and ran through money easily. That was motive for taking the cash, but it wasn't proof. After speaking to him, she was hopeful that he wasn't involved. She'd gotten pretty good at reading faces, and even though their conversation hadn't been in person, she'd still been able to pick up on his body language when he answered her questions. Ward had been forthright and didn't seem to have anything to hide.

At that point, Hannah was about ready to toss everything in the air and base her suspicions on where the papers fell. There was good reason to suspect everyone, but there was just as much reasonable evidence to dismiss each of them from the list.

There weren't many options left unless she considered the storage company, the grumpy neighbor, or absolutely anyone in the crowd. Of course, there was no way of tracing the entire audience after fifty years. The grumpy neighbor was dead, and everyone said he was more bluster than action anyway. Based on what she knew of his descendant, Hannah was inclined to agree.

Hannah had to admit, she was suddenly feeling a bit more sympathetic toward Sheriff Crane. There were either no other suspects, or the hundreds of people who had visited the festival. This felt like a wild-goose chase, and she was starting to doubt her chances of solving it.

She closed her eyes and continued to stroke the dog's soft fur as she debated her next step. The rhythmic motion soothed her, and from Smoky's contented sounds, it seemed a mutual feeling. "What do you think, Smoky? I'm beginning to understand why the sheriff wanted to blame it on a person who could never be found."

Hannah felt her thoughts drifting. She had no idea how much time had passed when she was jolted awake by Archer Lestrade's teasing voice.

"Well, what do you know? Liam, I think Smoky has taken your place in Hannah's heart."

"Who could blame her?" Liam replied mournfully. "That dog is cuter than is good for him—or for me."

Hannah blinked and yawned. When her vision cleared, three grimy firefighters stood over her. She had eyes only for one, and the first thing she noticed was how weary he looked. Archer and Colt also seemed exhausted, and her heart went out to these brave men. "I heard the fire trucks go out earlier this morning. Was the fire that bad?"

Liam nodded. "Turns out your suspicions were correct. The fires were connected to the festival."

His words cleared the last vestiges of sleep from Hannah's mind, which now flooded with visions of the festival being ruined. "What happened? How bad is the damage?" She cut herself off. "No, wait. You must all be exhausted. I have lunch for you in the kitchen. Why don't I go get it ready while you clean up?"

Grateful smiles greeted her words. Archer and Colt immediately headed for the showers, but Liam extended a hand to help her up. "I'll tell you all about it while we eat, okay? But the festival will be fine. We contained the damage."

Hannah breathed a sigh of relief. "Thank you. This is not something I wanted to be right about."

"I know." He looked at her with love shining through the fatigue in his eyes. "Right now, I would love nothing more than a Hannah hug. But I'm too filthy for that, so how about a kiss for your smoky fiancé?" He shot a playful glare at the dog. "Don't get any ideas, Smoky."

Hannah cupped his chin in her hands and swiped a smudge with her thumb. "How about a kiss for my favorite fiancé?" she asked as she leaned in.

Liam kissed her, then drew back and held out his hand. "Phone, please."

Hannah laughed. "What will it be this time?"

"Smoky can keep his name." Liam winked at her, then started to type in his new designation. "I prefer being your favorite."

Hannah chuckled when she saw that his contact info now read, *Liam "My Favorite Fiancé" Berthold*. "Always."

Colt and Archer approached from down the hall, so Liam reluctantly pulled away. "I'd better clean up."

Hannah caught his hand as he started to turn. She held up her phone. "Soon it will say husband."

Liam's smile was warm with promise. "Can't wait."

With a song in her heart, Hannah headed back to the kitchen. She had hungry firemen to feed.

The trio came into the kitchen and settled around the table where Hannah had set out an array of sandwiches and salads. Good thing she'd brought extra, because the guys were clearly ravenous after their long morning.

After wolfing down his sandwich, Archer was the first to speak. "Make Liam say it again, Hannah. You were right."

Hannah fought a smile. "Is that what you say to Bryn?"

Archer's eyes widened at the idea of saying such a thing to his spunky fiancée.

"Burn!" Colt laughed.

Liam pushed back his empty plate and wiped his mouth. "That really hit the spot, Hannah. Thank you. Archer's right, though. I should have listened to you."

Hannah shook it off. "It was a worry, but I had no proof."

"You've got good instincts, and I should know to trust them by now."

"So what happened? Why are you sure it's connected to the festival?"

"They burned the ticket booth," Colt answered.

Hannah gasped.

Liam took her hand. "Set it up to look just like the fire in 1976. Fortunately, we do know who it was. Colin has them cooling their feet in the jail right now."

Hannah leaned forward. "So? Don't keep me in suspense. Who was it?"

Chapter Twenty-Three

The air buzzed at the Hot Spot on Friday night. The energy was electric. Part of it was the incoming weather front, but most of it was the news of the morning's fire and it being the final night before the festival would begin. Excited chatter filled the crowded room. Hannah and her team had prepared for a large turnout, but the line was out the door as they tried to keep up with all the people willing to wait for a table.

Since the weather was potentially dangerous, Junior and his friends had reserved an early table and then stuck around for an extended jam session. This complicated Hannah's attempts to turn over tables because none of the diners wanted to leave when they could stay for a free concert. She didn't want to alienate patrons who were already dining, nor turn away those who had made reservations. The Hot Spot simply wasn't large enough to accommodate everyone who wanted to be there. It was a good sort of problem, but still one that needed to be resolved.

Dylan turned out to be the one with a brilliant solution. After a table of diners finished dessert, he handed out flyers for the festival and encouraged them to come support Blackberry Valley and see more of the music if they'd enjoyed this preview. Since he was clearing away their dishes as he said it, they were left with little choice but to move on, yet they did so with a smile as they chatted about buying tickets to the festival.

Hannah made a point of congratulating Dylan. “That was amazing. You just ushered all those people out the door and made them happy about it.”

She was laughing, but Dylan blushed. “It was easy. They liked the music. I just told them how to hear more of it.”

Hannah could have burst with pride about how far Dylan had come since she’d first hired him. Going back to school had been good for him, but she liked to think that working here had boosted him in ways book learning never could. Every member of her staff was valuable to her, but they all had a soft spot for Dylan.

Once Dylan moved on to clear another table, Hannah headed back to the kitchen to pick up another tray of food to deliver, and to tell Jacob to expect a new rush of orders. For most of the evening, she had been kept running, but that hadn’t stopped her mind from dwelling on the news Liam had dropped. At every table she passed, she heard conversations about the narrowly averted disaster with that morning’s fire.

After Liam, Archer, and Colt had revealed the culprits, Liam had accompanied Hannah to a hastily called meeting of the festival committee. Everyone was on edge, even though the perpetrators had been caught. The reason was pretty clear. The young men Colin had arrested were just teenagers—but they were members of the Hughes family. Apparently the feud was alive and well and worth fighting in their minds. The question that hung like a pall over the festival preparations was whether or not there were other family members who wanted to escalate.

Hannah shook her head as she set a tray down. She didn't understand feuds to begin with, but the utter pointlessness of old feuds being reignited after fifty years seemed like a complete waste of time and effort.

She reached the table of hungry people and handed off her tray of meals to Raquel in exchange for one stacked with dirty dishes. This was an all-hands-on-deck kind of dinner rush, but it seemed to finally be winding down. As Hannah headed back to the kitchen, she wondered what Maureen would have to say about the afternoon's news. Wasn't this exactly the part of her family legacy that she'd been trying to escape?

Hannah set the dishes on the counter and was loading them into the dishwasher when she heard the kitchen phone extension ring. When it continued to ring without Elaine answering out front, Jacob picked up and gave the standard Hot Spot greeting but added on, "Chef Jacob speaking."

When Jacob repeated the greeting and then hung up in annoyance, Hannah's nerves kicked in. Were these hang-up calls also related to the feud? She couldn't imagine how, but maybe she should have mentioned them to the sheriff. She tried to think what day they'd begun, and if that had coincided with the jam sessions. Liam said she had good instincts, and currently they were flashing warning lights.

Colin had promised to call on the neighboring towns for some extra patrols, but Hannah was still jumpy, so when the phone rang again, she dashed for it without waiting for Elaine to pick up. "Hello, Hot Spot, Hannah speaking."

"Why, hello, Hannah. I'm not used to you answering. It's Jack Delaney. I was hoping Elaine could squeeze me in somewhere later. I can bring those newspaper issues with me if she can."

Hannah let out a breath. "Sure, Jack. We're packed to the rafters, but I'm sure we can find room for you. You didn't by any chance just call and get cut off, did you?"

"No," he said, sounding puzzled.

Hannah managed not to groan aloud. "Okay, I thought maybe the phone was glitching. I'll give Elaine a heads-up, and we'll see you when you get here."

She disconnected the call and shrugged at Jacob. "These hang-up calls are increasing. If it continues, I'm going to speak to the sheriff about them. But right now, I have to let Elaine know that Jack Delaney is going to drop by." She smiled despite her nerves. "I guess he liked your barbecue the other night. Do you have anything to take to the dining room?"

"No, this order needs a couple more minutes, but overall things are slowing, so it should be okay. I can breathe now."

"You're my hero. I'll check back in a bit."

"Do I have to apologize to Liam?" Jacob's laughter followed her out of the room.

"You're my *culinary* hero," she called over her shoulder as the doors swung closed behind her.

Elaine was back at the waitress stand, so Hannah made her way there and relayed Jack's message. The front door swung open, and Shelby Lowe entered. She looked around, a hesitant expression on her face, so Hannah stepped forward to greet her. "Hello, Shelby. Good to see you again. Are you here for dinner or just the music?"

Shelby glanced around uneasily. "Actually, I was hoping to talk to you. I didn't even think about how crowded your restaurant would be."

From the woman's anxious manner, Hannah sensed that something was not right. Since she had intended to speak to Martin Lowe's widow anyway and the line of waiting diners had finally all been seated and served, Hannah took Elaine aside and asked her to hold down the fort for a bit. Elaine assured her she was fine and promised to check in if anything changed.

"Why don't we step outside, Mrs. Lowe? It will be more private there."

Shelby agreed, and the two women exited the restaurant.

"Would you prefer to walk or find a bench somewhere?"

"If we can walk slowly, I think I would prefer that. I may lose my nerve if we stop."

That comment sparked Hannah's interest even more. Intrigued, she started to head down Main Street. "How can I help you, Shelby?"

Shelby grimaced. "I have something to share, and I don't know who to talk to. The sheriff would be the obvious choice, but my previous experience leaves me wary of that."

Hannah briefly wondered if she was the one who needed a bench. This was her third conversation today in which someone had chosen her as their confidante. It was flattering, but more than a little overwhelming. A sudden thought occurred to her. "Have you been calling the Hot Spot and hanging up?"

The elderly woman dipped her head. "I'm mortified to admit it, but yes. As I said, I needed to speak with you, but each time a different employee answered the phone, and the time you picked up I lost my nerve. But Beverly Conley told me I could trust you."

Hannah sucked in a breath. Was this something Beverly had just learned that morning?

Shelby suddenly clutched Hannah's arm. "Maybe I do need to sit."

She'd grown pale, so Hannah guided her along the sidewalk. "There's a bench just up ahead."

Once they were seated, Hannah waited for Shelby to catch her breath, but she could see the woman was close to hyperventilating. Time to intervene. "Shelby, if Beverly thought you should talk to me, I'm going to guess this has to do with the theft of the festival proceeds."

"How did you know?" The whispered words were so faint that Hannah could barely hear them over a breeze rustling the leaves.

"That is the part of the mystery I have yet to solve, so it stands to reason. You can tell me what you know, and then we'll figure out what to do, okay? I promise to help however I can. Now I want you to take a breath and hold it until I tell you to let it out. We'll do it together."

Hannah walked Shelby through some paced breathing until the color came back into her cheeks and she was able to breathe easily on her own. Hannah glanced along the street. The sun had set behind the stormy clouds, and streetlights illuminated the deserted Main Street now. There was no one to overhear whatever Shelby might say.

"Whenever you're ready, I'm here to help."

Shelby took another shaky breath and then spoke in a rush of words. "You're right that it is about the money. Fifty years ago my husband stole the proceeds from the concert." Her breath hitched, but she continued. "I didn't know it at the time, but he told me on his deathbed. He said he'd made a mistake because he was so angry at the boys for letting it all get out of hand and ruin his life. In the moment, he felt he was entitled to compensation because the band was breaking up, and he thought he was about to lose everything. But guilt haunted him for the rest of his life. He wanted to make amends but couldn't figure out how, since the festival was long over."

Hannah let the news settle. Most of the pieces were in place now. Junior's theory that someone had found the mandolin and taken that and the money hadn't panned out. The reality was that the mandolin had probably been in the box Junior left it in until the storage company packed everything up. And there it had stayed until Beverly shared the memorabilia with Evangeline.

Martin Lowe was dead, so there didn't seem to be anything to be gained by exposing his crime, but that decision would be up to the sheriff. She started to say as much, but Shelby cut her off.

"That is not the part I need your help with. My Martin did not set the fire in the ticket booth, so it was not done to cover the theft, as everyone suspected. Martin said he would never have done something like that because it risked too many lives if it got out of hand." Shelby paused to sniff and wipe away a tear. "Martin was a decent man who made a mistake. I'm not denying that what he did was a crime, but there was someone else involved. As I said, Martin did not set the fire, but he was blackmailed by whoever did. Someone saw him take that money, and they made sure he paid for it for the rest of his life."

Shelby had to stop to compose herself again. In the silence, Hannah's mind raced with questions, but Shelby wasn't done with her story. She began again, and her voice was steadier.

"I didn't learn the extent of the blackmail until after Martin died. When I was going through his papers, I found the letters. They weren't signed, but there was one sent just a day before he had the heart attack that killed him. The person threatened to expose everything if he didn't deposit $100,000 in a designated account."

Hannah gasped at the amount.

"I hired a private detective, but he was unable to trace the letters or the account owner. I had given up hope of finding out the blackmailer's identity, but when Arthur's grandson decided to revive this festival, it seemed like a new chance. I want to know who the person is, and this time I want them to pay. Will you help me?"

Chapter Twenty-Four

Hannah settled back against the bench, speechless. She knew Shelby was waiting for answers now, but it would take some time to wrap her head around this. No wonder Sheriff Crane had been unable to solve the mystery. It sprouted in new directions every time she turned around.

"Do you have any reason to believe the person who sent the notes was connected to the festival?"

"I have no evidence, but it stands to reason it would have to have been someone who saw him take it, hence the connection to the festival."

Hannah thought of Sheriff Crane's conclusion that any one of the hundreds of fans in attendance could have stolen the mandolin. The same could be said of anyone witnessing the theft. Hannah couldn't imagine how she could locate the blackmailer when a private detective hadn't been successful, but the grief-stricken widow watched her with such a hopeful expression that Hannah didn't know how to turn down her request.

"Do you have the blackmail notes?"

"I do." Shelby reached into her bag and removed a manila envelope.

Hannah opened it and pulled out the first letter. Her blood ran cold at the clearly stated threat. She quickly glanced at the other notes before putting them back in the envelope. She took a moment to pray before responding.

"Shelby, I'm afraid I can't make any promises, and I do have to get back to my restaurant, but if you will let me keep these for tonight, I promise to look through them more closely and see if I can find any clues to help you. Are you okay with that?"

Shelby let out a soft rush of breath and lifted her eyes to hold Hannah's gaze. "I know I am asking the impossible, but if you will try, that is all I can hope for. If it is God's will, you will find the person who caused my husband's death, and I will be at peace."

Shelby's words weighed heavily on Hannah as they walked back to the restaurant, and for the rest of the evening as the Hot Spot crowd thinned and the music died away.

Liam was keeping watch out at the campgrounds tonight. Once Hannah and her team had cleaned up and she had locked the door, she took the packet of blackmail letters and climbed the stairs to her apartment. As she opened the door to the silent, empty living room, she wished she had Smoky to keep her company again.

After brewing a cup of chamomile and lavender tea that she hoped would prove soothing, she sat at her table and opened the envelope. She pulled out the letters, twenty in all, and spread them on the table. The first thing she noticed was that both the quality of the paper and the style of type had changed over time. There were dates on the back of each, but Hannah suspected that was Martin's way of keeping track, since the dates were handwritten. Using that information, she arranged them in chronological order, and a pattern emerged.

The very first note had been sent in 1976, shortly after the festival ended. For the first few years, they arrived like clockwork, two a year—one in early December and one in late June. The demands started out fairly low. The first one was for only fifty dollars, which would translate to just shy of $300 in today's money. As the years went by, the demand increased dramatically. That seemed to match what Hannah remembered about the trajectory of Ward's career, which would have meant increased wealth for his manager.

As Hannah came to the final demand, she focused on something Shelby had said. This last note had arrived shortly before Martin died. It would seem there had been no effort made to extort his widow. Hannah couldn't be sure if that was significant or not, but she retrieved her notebook and recorded the observation.

Hannah rubbed her tired eyes and stared down at the papers again. She really didn't know what she could possibly find here. The weight of Shelby's expectations kept her reading and rereading long after she should have been in bed, but she finally gave up. Maybe fresh eyes in the daylight would see something she was missing now.

She sent a good-night text to Liam and got ready for bed. After she had finished her evening prayers, climbed into bed, and turned out the light, she whispered a final prayer. The festival was supposed to begin Saturday afternoon, and she prayed that the weather would improve, the feuding Hughes family would stay away, and all would go smoothly.

When watery sunlight woke Hannah from a restless night, she considered trying to bury her face in the pillow, but the mystery of the blackmail notes preyed on her mind as it had all night. Fighting off a yawn, she rose and stumbled to the kitchen and the coffeepot. While the coffee brewed, she dragged herself under a hot shower, hoping to wash away the cobwebs.

Her brain felt clearer but still empty of solutions as she poured her coffee and took a sip before returning to the table to study the notes she'd left there. A drop of coffee ran down the side of the mug, and she caught it with her thumb before it could land on the paper.

That was when it hit her.

Whether it was the caffeine kicking in or just a fresh perspective, Hannah didn't know, but she suddenly saw what she had missed the previous evening—a coffee stain on the edge of one of the notes. A chill of premonition shivered through her as an idea clicked into focus.

She quickly grabbed her phone and pulled up the photos of the police files that she'd snapped. Then she turned to the box of files Maureen had loaned her. The final clue kicked in when Hannah retrieved the photo of Maureen flirting with the sheriff. She held an unmistakable paper cup in her hand. It could have held something else, but Hannah would bet the moon that it was the coffee the reporter had claimed to be addicted to.

That addiction might just be the key to her downfall.

Hannah paced the apartment as she sipped her own coffee, trying to order her thoughts and figure out what to do. She could call the sheriff, but she only had her suspicions, not concrete proof, and he was dealing with Maureen's relatives anyway. That would also keep Liam tied up today as they protected the audience.

Hannah let out an exasperated sigh. She was smart enough not to go alone, and there was no way she was going to involve Lacy in something risky at this point in her pregnancy.

Hannah picked up her phone and called Monroe, who answered with a groggy voice. “Good morning, Hannah.”

“I need your help. Can you get away this morning?” Hannah heard some fumbling noises in the background before Monroe finally responded.

“I’m supposed to have a final rehearsal before I perform with my mom at three when the festival opens, but we can skip that if it’s important.”

“Does blowing open the whole mystery count as important?”

“I’ll pick you up in half an hour. But Hannah, I’m going to need details.”

“You’ll have plenty of time to catch up. We’re going to Nashville.”

Chapter Twenty-Five

"Does this trip have anything to do with my grandfather's mandolin?"

Monroe wasted no time in getting to the point when she picked Hannah up in her red convertible. Hannah hadn't been thrilled about taking Monroe's car, but her friend insisted that she was the one familiar with Nashville. Hannah cast a worried glance at the threatening sky as she considered how to answer. "No, this is about the stolen money, but don't worry about the mandolin."

Monroe started to interrupt her, but Hannah waved her off. "I know what happened to the mandolin, and your grandfather will hear the truth today."

The car swerved as Monroe reacted. "Hannah! You can't leave me hanging like that."

"Keep your eyes on the road. I know you want answers. That's why I was trying not to bring it up. I'm truly sorry, but it's not my story to share."

Monroe bit her lower lip and concentrated on the road. "Will you just tell me if it involves Nana?"

"I can promise you it does not."

With that assurance, Monroe exhaled sharply. "I was afraid your visit yesterday had something to do with it. Nana's anxiety has been through the roof, but since your visit, she's seemed calmer."

Hannah realized that the change in Beverly's behavior probably had to do with unloading her secret, but that might not have been everything. "She also had a visit with Shelby Lowe after we spoke. I ran into Shelby on my way out and asked how she and Beverly had remained friends all these years despite the feud and the band's breakup. Shelby told me that they valued their friendship too much to allow it to be broken by 'foolishness that should have been worked through.'"

Monroe smiled. "She's a wise woman. I know Nana was looking forward to her visit. I'm glad it was a good one."

"So how are you doing? Have you made any decisions about your life and career?"

"No. We've been so busy, I've barely had time to think about it. But I've had a chance to get to know Harry White this week. We've had some interesting discussions about how men can share the same concerns."

"Do I detect some romantic interest?"

A smile blossomed on Monroe's face. "Maybe? One of our discussions did revolve around the benefits of a relationship with someone in the industry who understands the expectations and stresses as well as the highs that come from performing, or, in his case, creating the show." Suddenly her glow dimmed. "Please tell me Harry and his family are not involved in this. I know his dad was one of the original suspects, so I've been a bit wary of getting involved if it would hurt Grandpa Eddie."

Now it was Hannah's turn to smile. "I can promise you that Harry's family was not involved." Monroe's evident relief gave

Hannah more of a clue about the burgeoning romance than her words had. "I'm happy for you, Monroe."

"Don't get too excited yet. It's early days, but he invited me to join a small festival he's working on in Northern California in August. I'll admit, I was worried about accepting if things were still tense around here with Nana and Grandpa Eddie, but you've been hinting that might be resolved soon. Right?"

"I can tell you that at least two of the mysteries are solved. I'm hoping we can solve the third on our trip today."

"There are three mysteries?"

"Well, there's the big one of what happened during the 1976 festival, but it turns out there wasn't just one answer."

Hannah wanted to avoid discussing anything else about the mysteries, especially because she realized that in all the chaos yesterday, she'd touched base with Colin, so she turned the conversation back. "Monroe, as your friend, I have one bit of relationship advice based on experience. Don't let doubts stop you from pursuing this chance with Harry if you really like him."

"Did you do that with Liam?"

"Let's say I wasted too much time stuck in the past and almost missed out on the best thing that's ever happened to me. I used work as an excuse because I was scared." Hannah laughed to lighten the mood. "Learn from my mistakes—unlike the time you decided to follow me jumping off the monkey bars and ended up with a broken ankle."

Monroe laughed along with her. "Mom was so mad at me for that. And I spent the summer unable to swim." Her expression grew soft. "It turned out to be a good thing, though. Grandpa Eddie took pity on me. That's the summer he taught me how to play guitar."

They reminisced about days gone by and caught up on their adult lives until the highway sign indicated they were ten miles from Nashville. Monroe abruptly changed the topic. "Am I just the chauffeur, or do I have a role to play in this meeting?"

"I was thinking about that. I want to sort of open the discussion in a casual way to lead her into an admission of what I think she did. She might be less defensive if we focus on you as Eddie's granddaughter. I'll introduce you and explain that you wanted to meet her because she knew your grandpa back in the day."

"I do." Monroe paused. "I know you can't tell me who stole Grandpa Eddie's mandolin, but did Maureen really have nothing to do with it? I'm not a good enough actress to fangirl if she had a part in hurting him."

"She had nothing to do with that part. I could be wrong, but I really don't think she knows what happened to the mandolin. There was certainly nothing in any of her articles to hint at it."

There had been nothing in Maureen's articles to indicate she knew and intended to blackmail the person who stole the money either, but Hannah had to assume Junior also would have heard from her if she'd known what he had done.

"So I should just be Eddie's granddaughter who's curious to meet someone who knew him back when he was performing?"

"Yes. I'm not trying to be secretive, but I don't want to share my suspicion in case I'm wrong. Can you try to follow my lead?"

"Yes ma'am." Monroe saluted playfully.

"Eyes on the road," Hannah cautioned her. "Remind me never to take a road trip with you. Should I put the address in the GPS?"

"Not necessary. I've lived here for most of my adult life, so I should be able to find it on my own."

Hannah gave her the address, and they pulled up outside Maureen's house fifteen minutes later.

"Is she expecting us?"

"Yes, but she doesn't know why." Hannah climbed out of the car and retrieved a bakery box from where she'd tucked it safely under the seat. "She loved the jam cake last time, so I brought another one to guarantee our welcome."

Monroe giggled. "You certainly know what you're doing." She looked up at the sky. "I don't like the looks of those clouds, so help me pull up the roof before we go in, okay?"

The two friends secured the convertible's roof, then headed up the front walk. Hannah rang the bell. She was surprised when Hilary answered. Had she stayed home today because Hannah was coming?

"Hello again," Hilary greeted Hannah. She did a double take when she saw Monroe.

Hannah made the introduction. "Living in Nashville, you probably know my friend, Monroe Taylor."

"I've seen her perform," Hilary replied to Hannah before turning to Monroe. "I loved your music when you performed with your mother, but your solo stuff is my favorite."

Monroe thanked her for the compliment, and Hilary ushered them back to the library where Maureen was waiting. "Look what Hannah brought—another jam cake, just like you hoped." She turned to Hannah. "I think you won a special place in her heart with that on your first visit."

Hannah pasted on a smile in response, but she knew that special place was about to be obliterated when she called Maureen out for blackmail.

Hannah set the box on the table, and they made small talk about Monroe and her connection to Eddie Conley for a while. Hilary seemed more starstruck than her mother, and Hannah wondered if Maureen had figured out the reason for her return. Her suspicion was confirmed when Maureen sent Hilary off to cut the cake and bring them coffee.

She turned an assessing eye on Hannah once her daughter was gone. "I'm sure introducing my daughter and me to Eddie's granddaughter was not your primary reason for this visit. Why don't you tell me why you're really here before Hilary returns?" Maureen looked physically frail sitting in her recliner under a blanket, but there was a glint of steel in her eyes.

In that moment, Hannah realized there was no sign of the welcoming, generous woman she and Lacy had visited. Today Hannah was face-to-face with the ambitious reporter who had been willing to blackmail her way out of the holler. She cut right to the chase. "I think you know why I'm here. I had a visit from Shelby Lowe yesterday. She's in Blackberry Valley for the festival."

"That's nice for her," Maureen replied as she picked at a thread on the blanket. "But I'm not sure I know who she is."

Hannah had to give Maureen credit. She was holding her nerve well. Apparently this was going to be a chess match.

Hannah sat back in her chair and studied the older woman, watching to see what reaction she would get with her next words. "I don't know if you would've met her, but I'm sure you knew her husband, Martin."

Finally a flicker in Maureen's eyes betrayed her.

Hannah continued. "Martin has been gone many years now, as I'm sure you know, but Shelby has kept some of his papers. She brought them to me."

Maureen was a worthy opponent. Her face was hard as flint as she retorted, "Fifty years seems like a long time to hang on to worthless papers."

Out of the corner of her eye, Hannah saw Hilary come around the corner, balancing a tray of coffee and cake.

"Oh, but they're not really so worthless, are they, Maureen?" Hannah said. "Not when they're the clue to understanding what happened to the money that was stolen from the festival."

"They don't prove anything," Maureen stated defiantly, seemingly unaware of what she had just admitted.

"Mother, I think perhaps it's time for Hannah to leave," Hilary said.

Maureen scowled at her daughter. "You don't need to protect me. It's been fifty years. This is all bluster. There's no proof. Give me my coffee."

"No proof of what?" Hilary asked as she dutifully poured the coffee and handed the cup to her mother. "What is she talking about?"

No one spoke.

Hilary's voice sharpened as she glared at Hannah. "I don't know what I missed, but the last time you visited, my mother was generous in answering your questions and sharing her files with you. Surely you're not trying to claim that there's anything in those files proving she did something wrong. That would be incredibly impolite."

Hannah kept her eyes on Maureen as she responded. "Do you consider blackmail impolite?"

Maureen's expression didn't change, but Hilary gasped. "I've gone through those files myself. There's nothing about blackmail in there."

Hannah continued to watch Maureen while she spoke to Hilary. "I guess your mother didn't keep carbon copies of the notes she sent to Martin Lowe."

Hilary's expression morphed into one Hannah could easily picture in a courtroom. "Say nothing, Mother."

Maureen flapped a hand at her. "Don't bother yourself, Hilary. It was fifty years ago. It doesn't matter any longer."

Hannah had done her research, and she pulled the facts out now. "Fortunately, that's not quite true. In Kentucky, blackmail is considered theft by extortion. It's a felony, and might even be a federal crime in this instance, since it crossed state lines. As a lawyer, I believe Hilary can confirm that there is no statute of limitations on felonies in Kentucky."

Hilary had grown quite pale, and Hannah felt sorry for her. Obviously she'd been unaware of what her mother had done.

"How did you guess?" Maureen's once-defiant voice had become weak and shaky. The coffee cup shook in her trembling hands, spilling coffee onto her pristine blanket.

Hannah gentled her voice. "The coffee stains gave you away."

Hilary set her coffee aside and stood. "Mother, do not say another word. Ms. Prentiss, I believe you and your friend have overstayed your welcome."

Hannah set aside her cup and rose. "I'm sorry it has come to this. We will leave, but your mother should be prepared for a visit from the sheriff."

"Oh, my goodness, you were amazing in there, Hannah. Did you ever want to be a lawyer?"

Hannah would have laughed, but her heart was heavy. "I was really hoping she would feel remorse. Was it me, or did she seem almost proud?"

"Yes, at least until you started spouting legalese. Did she start the fire too?"

"I think so. Did you hear that it was relatives of hers who have been setting the fires out at the festival grounds?" Monroe nodded, so Hannah continued. "Shelby said Martin absolutely did not set the fire. It stands to reason that Maureen did it to push the idea that the cash was all burned up. That would have discouraged an investigation." Hannah made a face. "You know, I initially thought she had cozied up to the sheriff to get information for her story, but it was probably the reverse. She was feeding him the narrative."

"What are you going to do now?"

"First, I'm going to call Sheriff Steele. He'll probably be annoyed at me for coming out here, but he's had his hands full, and I needed the truth before I could proceed with explaining about your grandfather's mandolin."

"Are you going to tell me about that now?"

"No, I'm going to let the person who knows what happened tell your grandfather first."

Hannah took out her phone and texted Liam. MYSTERY SOLVED. MONROE AND I ARE ON OUR WAY BACK FROM SEEING MAUREEN. LONG STORY, BUT FIRES RUN IN THE FAMILY.

Liam texted back immediately. CAN'T WAIT. BE CAREFUL. THERE ARE FLASH FLOOD WARNINGS IN EFFECT.

WILL DO, BUT IT'S NOT EVEN RAINING HERE.

Next Hannah placed a call to Colin. Vanessa answered and told Hannah he was busy with the Hughes brothers and their attorney, but she would relay Hannah's call request.

Hannah had no sooner disconnected that call than her phone rang again with a number she didn't recognize. She picked up. "Hello?"

"Hannah, it's Hilary Wright. I was hoping we could talk."

"I think you and your mother would be better off talking to a criminal lawyer and the sheriff, not to me."

"But you're the one who came to talk to my mother. Who better than you?"

Hannah wanted to reiterate that she needed a lawyer and the sheriff, but there was a pang in Hilary's voice that touched her. She tried to imagine herself in Hilary's position, but it was impossible. Her own mother would never have gotten involved in such a scheme.

"Hannah, please. There are some things you should know."

"Monroe and I are already on our way home."

There was silence on the other end of the connection for a minute. "We have a summer house out on the river. You'll pass it on your way. Meet me there? Please. I won't keep you long." After a pause, Hilary pushed her plea. "She's the villain to you, but she's my mother. She's all I have."

Monroe, who was clearly eavesdropping on the conversation, briefly laid a hand on Hannah's arm. "Ask her for directions."

Chapter Twenty-Six

"This is like every bad horror movie where the innocent girl opens the door while you're covering your eyes and screaming, 'Don't do it!'"

Monroe burst into laughter. "I don't remember you being this dramatic." She parked at the cabin Hilary had directed them to. "She's a woman defending her mother, not a serial-killer clown."

That comment drew a matching laugh from Hannah, but she still had a sense of foreboding. "I'll hear her out, but I'm texting Liam and the sheriff to let them know." She shook her head as she typed the messages. "They're both going to be furious with me." She shot a pointed look at Monroe. "With us."

"Just remind them they'd do the same for their mothers."

"You do realize that doesn't even make sense, right? Hilary's mother is the criminal who ruined lives."

"We all make mistakes, Hannah. We're all sinners. The least we can do is hear Hilary's explanation."

The first fat raindrops hit the convertible's windshield. "Liam warned that there's a flash flood warning."

"I'll keep an eye on the weather. Hilary must have broken all the speed limits because here she is."

A flashy silver sports car pulled up beside them. Hilary jumped out and held up a hand for them to wait while she dashed ahead and opened the cabin. Once the door was unlocked and the lights switched on, she called to them to come in.

Hannah was still full of misgivings, but she hadn't backed down from solving a mystery yet, so she stiffened her spine and resolved to see this one through.

"I'm sorry it's a bit chilly. We haven't used the place yet this year," Hilary explained as she ushered them inside. "Momma has a cleaning service keep it ready, so I can offer coffee." She winced. "Or maybe you'd prefer tea."

Hannah looked to Monroe, who gave a subtle shake of her head. "Thank you but no, Hilary. We'd rather just get on with this. We have a longish drive, and the forecast is bad."

"Then please come sit and listen."

Hannah and Monroe followed her into a lovely room with huge glass windows overlooking the river. Floral-upholstered sofas and chairs created a welcome retreat.

"What a pretty room. It's a far cry from the rustic cabin I would have expected as a river retreat," Monroe said.

Hilary waited as they settled on the sofa facing her. She drew a breath, exhaled slowly, and began. "That is part of the story. My mother came from a very poor family in the Kentucky hills. From things she has said, I know that life was really hard. She barely spoke of it. I remember having to do a family tree in elementary school. Mom wouldn't tell me anything. Told me to focus on my father's side of the family. That didn't satisfy my teacher, so I did some research on my own, looked things up, read some local newspapers. Her father was a hard man, an intolerant man. As an adult, I learned more because she wrote about it in her memoir. I assume you know of that from your investigation."

Hannah nodded slowly. "I know that the Hughes family feuded with the Blackberry Mountain Boys, especially Ward's family, and tried to ruin the festivals. I also know that Sheriff Steele currently has three of her relatives sitting in jail for starting fires to disrupt this year's festival."

Hilary sank back against the cushions and covered her face. "I'm very sorry to hear that. I'd hoped the feuding was over and done with after all these years. But, Hannah, that should show you the kind of blood she came from. She was desperate to escape. I think in that desperation, she was unable to distinguish between right and wrong. She only saw a way out."

Conflicting emotions welled in Hannah. "I understand all of that, Hilary. And I saw the gracious woman she can be when I visited the first time, but that doesn't change the fact that she committed serious crimes. In trying to rescue herself, she ruined a man's life."

"A man who had committed a crime of his own and gave her the opening to ruin his life. I know two wrongs don't make a right, but my mother is an old woman now. The idea of her spending her last days in a prison cell breaks my heart."

Hannah struggled with what she wanted to say. "I understand, and if she was my mother, I'd be saying the same. But you saw the way she reacted today, Hilary. She didn't express an ounce of remorse for what she did."

"I think that's her fear talking. Whenever she feels threatened, the hardscrabble girl emerges."

"Hilary, you're a lawyer, so you know better than to ask me to withhold evidence." Hannah held Hilary's gaze. "I will talk to my friend the sheriff. I will explain the evidence and the circumstances. I don't know how he will react, but I know he will have to speak with the county prosecutor, who will decide. This is not my call, but I imagine if you got your mother a good criminal attorney, they could fight for leniency."

Monroe caught Hannah's eye as she pointed at the window. The sight of rain pouring down matched the sudden drumming on the roof. "Hilary, does this river flood?"

"Only when there's flash flooding." She followed the direction of Hannah's gaze and reacted to the rising water. "We should probably leave. I'm sorry. But Hannah, please promise you will try to help my mother."

As Hannah followed Monroe's dash for the car, she once again wished they'd brought her trusty Subaru. The rutted road they'd followed to the river house suddenly looked like a field of mud. "Do you think we'd be better off waiting it out here than trying to drive in the mud?"

"This car has seen me through plenty of tough weather," Monroe replied. "She's more reliable than she looks."

Hannah hoped so. The rain was coming down harder with every passing moment. "Monroe, I don't have a good feeling about this."

Monroe gunned the car to push through a sloppy stretch. "I have an even worse feeling about staying put. That house was right on the riverbank, and I've seen too many videos lately of houses being washed away."

"Let's say a prayer for our safety and for everyone in the path of the storm. I'll lead. You keep your eyes on the road."

They prayed and then Monroe said, "You know the old saying. Singing is like praying twice." She began to sing, "My Hope Is Built on Nothing Less."

Hannah sang along, but she kept an eye out for Hilary. They should have waited to make sure she followed.

They rounded a bend. Monroe slammed on the brakes and skidded to a stop.

The road they'd driven along earlier was submerged in deep, rushing water. There was no way to get across it safely.

Monroe shifted gears and tried to back up, but the car's tires spun in the mud. She turned to Hannah. They were stuck, and the water was rising fast.

"I think we have to try to get out and walk back," Hannah said. The rain was steadily increasing in strength, and the angry water could easily wash the convertible away if it got high enough.

Monroe closed her eyes and patted the steering wheel. "I don't want to abandon my baby, but…" The car shifted sideways. "We can't risk our lives over a car." She rolled down the window and stuck her head out. "The water is already up over the tires on my side. We have to climb out the passenger side. You go first and hang on to the door. Once you're out, I'll climb over the console and follow you."

As soon as Hannah opened the door, muddy water poured into the car and filled the well around her feet. "The current is so strong. I don't know how we're going to stand against it." Panic coursed through her. Was this one of those moments she'd heard about, where her life would flash before her eyes?

But she wasn't seeing her past. All she could think of was Liam, their upcoming wedding, and how she had to make it to safety. "Is there anything in the car we could use to tie us together?"

Monroe pointed. "Look in the glove compartment. I have some straps in there that I use to keep things from blowing away if the roof is down."

Hannah dug in the glove box and pulled out several straps. She unraveled one and wrapped it around her waist. After snapping the buckle, she handed another one to Monroe who locked it around her waist. Then they knotted the two together. "Climb over to my seat so you can get out if you must, but stay inside as long as it's safe. I'm going to try to reach a tree and use this other strap to tether us to it."

Monroe's voice shook as she agreed. "Hannah, I'm sorry I told you to agree to meeting with Hilary. We could have been halfway home by now."

"Or stuck somewhere else. We don't have time for regrets. We have to work as a team to get out of here now." Hannah tossed her phone to Monroe. "You call for help, then call Hilary and warn her while I try to get out." Hannah whispered a quick prayer and began to climb from the car. She set her right foot down in the water, then clung to the back door while she brought the other foot out. Water swirled around her legs, tugging her downhill, but Monroe held the strap firmly against the door, preventing her from sliding.

Hannah took a precious moment to study their surroundings. The copse of trees was farther than she'd hoped, but it was the only option. Every new cascade of water pushed the car closer to the edge, where the hillside had washed away.

She quickly buckled another strap to the first one and started to wade through the rushing torrent. It took every ounce of strength to fight the water, and she prayed for God's help to reach her goal.

Another swell of water crested above her on the hill and drove Hannah to her knees. She doggedly crawled forward, reaching for something, anything, beneath the water to latch on to. Inch by inch she pulled herself toward the trees.

"Hannah, a car is coming." Hannah could barely hear Monroe's voice over the wind and water. "It's Hilary."

Hannah peered up through the downpour. She clung to a rock with one hand and used the other to shove her sodden hair out of her face. At the top of the bend, she could see headlights. After a few moments, she saw the car door open and she could just make out Hilary walking toward them.

Was she here to help—or to watch them wash away, removing the threat to her mother?

Chapter Twenty-Seven

Hilary turned around and ran back to her car, taking Hannah's hope with her. But within moments Maureen's daughter was on her way back with a rope coiled around one arm. She walked until she was at the edge of the water, then cupped her hands around her mouth and called, "I'm going to tie the rope to my car and then throw it into the water. The current should carry it to you."

Hannah breathed a prayer of thanksgiving.

Hilary tossed the rope, but her first attempt fell short, and the rope floated out of Hannah's reach.

Hannah's arms burned with the effort of fighting the current and struggling to stay above water.

"I'm going to drown in here if I stay any longer," Monroe called from behind her. "I have to try to follow you now."

Hannah felt the straps slacken as Monroe moved. Hannah changed direction and crawled, trying to find something along what had been the side of the road to use as an anchor. She focused on the story of Jesus calling to Peter to walk on water. Surely her faith was strong enough that she could crawl through it.

"Hannah, I'm going to throw the rope again."

Hannah held her breath as the rope sailed toward them. But in her effort to reach them, Hilary had aimed too high, and the rope tangled in an overhanging branch. When Hilary yanked to free it, the rope broke the branch. Rope and branch plummeted into the water.

Hannah managed to avoid getting hit, but the swell of water caused by the impact hit her full in the face. She blinked as tears joined the water washing down her cheeks. "Dear Lord, help us."

Monroe yelled something behind her, but Hannah could barely hear as thunder roared. The storm was directly on top of them now. Monroe shouted again, and this time Hannah heard and relayed the message to Hilary. "Monroe says to throw the rope upstream so it will wash down to us."

Hilary coiled the rope again and then threw it. The wind caught it, and for a moment Hannah watched in helpless panic as it blew too far to the right. But then it hit the water, and the current carried the rope in her direction. She reached out and grasped the lifeline, holding it for all she was worth.

Back up the road, Hilary cheered. "I'll put the car in reverse and pull you out." She sprinted to her car.

Hannah struggled for breath, trying not to swallow any more floodwater as she checked on Monroe. "Are your knots secure?"

"Yes. I think the water made them swell, so they're holding."

"I think we should try to walk while she pulls us."

"Definitely."

Hannah heard the ignition catch, but then the car lurched toward them on the muddy slope. Hannah held her breath as Hilary kept gunning the engine. Slowly the car eased back along the road. The tension on the rope increased, and Hannah allowed it to pull her to her feet, then steadily toward safety. Around them, lightning flashed and thunder roared.

When Hannah's feet finally broke free of the water, she wanted to throw herself on the ground in exhaustion, but the danger wasn't over. She turned to help pull Monroe the remaining few feet to safety. With the final dregs of their energy, they scrambled to the safety of the car.

Hannah's fingers fumbled with the door handle, but she finally got it open and crawled into the back seat. Only when Monroe was safely beside her did she stop to unfasten the straps that had bound them together.

Hilary cranked up the car's heater, and Hannah and Monroe huddled together, shivering, sucking in gulps of air, all the time knowing they were only temporarily safe. Around them, the storm still thundered and water roared past, carrying shrubbery and other debris.

Hilary backed up the road until she could safely turn, but visibility was so limited that they decided it was best to just wait where they were until the storm eased.

Long, tense moments passed before Hannah spoke. "Thank you for the risks you took, Hilary. Without you..." Her voice fell away. She couldn't put into words the horror they had just avoided.

"Without me, you wouldn't have been in the situation to begin with," Hilary pointed out.

"You could have left us," Monroe said, echoing Hannah's earlier thoughts.

"Is that what you think? That I could just leave you to die so no one would know about my mother?" Hilary twisted in her seat to gape at them. "I realize neither of us has given you a reason to think highly of us, but my mother led a mostly good life and raised me with high moral standards. She made a terrible mistake and perpetuated it for years, but aside from that, she is a good person. I don't know how to explain the dichotomy other than the trauma of her childhood, because everything else she did in her life and career was about standing up for what was right."

Hannah nodded silently. "I truly hope the prosecutor will take that into account. I—"

"I see headlights!" Monroe interrupted.

Hannah and Hilary dropped their conversation and peered through the windshield. On the other side of the raging water they could see lights approaching. Hilary immediately flashed her high beams to warn of the danger, and in the light, Hannah saw a blue Jeep that she recognized. "It's Liam. How did he get here so fast? Monroe, do you still have my phone?"

Monroe fished it from her pocket. "Yes, but I doubt it works. I tried to protect both of our phones, but the water knocked me down."

"If you know his number, you can use mine," Hilary offered.

Hannah gratefully accepted the phone and punched in Liam's number. When his voice came on the line, everything hit her at once, and she could barely squeak out the words. "Liam, it's Hannah."

"Hannah, are you in Monroe's car?" His voice was tight with fear.

She saw the red convertible teetering on the edge of the abyss and understood Liam's question. "No, we're in Maureen's daughter's car. She's the one who flashed the lights at you."

Liam instructed them to stay in the car while he assessed the situation. According to the radar, the storm was expected to pass within the next ten minutes. He put in a call to the local fire department, and a truck soon arrived on scene, along with a tow truck to rescue Monroe's car. By the time Liam finished updating them on the situation, the flooding across the road had finally eased enough for him to reach Hannah.

She threw herself into his arms, and it was only when they closed around her that she finally felt safe. He held her as desperately as she clung to him. "Don't you ever scare me like that again," he whispered against her hair. "I've been calling and calling and getting no response."

"I'll try not to. My phone drowned in the flood. I'm so sorry I didn't heed your warning. I promise I will always listen to your advice."

At that, she felt a rumble of laughter from him. "I might have to put that into our vows, but I think it would be cruel to you. Not to mention unfair of me, when I love how headstrong you are." He pulled back far enough to kiss her, ignoring the whooping from Monroe and the firemen. "I love you, Hannah Prentiss."

"I love you too."

The tow truck driver approached them. "We're ready to head back with the car. The fire department is going to stay on-site until we can block off the damaged part of the road. You folks all okay to head back on your own?" He cast a doubtful look at Hannah.

"Just muddy and wet, but we'll be fine. Thank you so much."

The tow truck operator arranged with Monroe to take her car back to Nashville for repairs, and Liam and Hannah made sure Hilary was okay to drive home on her own. "We'll be in touch," Hannah said as Hilary started her car to drive away. "I promise I'll talk to the sheriff."

Once she had driven away, Hannah turned to Liam. "How did you know to come?"

"I saw your first text pop up while I was checking the radar. It looked bad, and I was not about to risk losing my fiancée. I hit the road immediately. I was more than halfway here by the time I got the second one."

Hannah hugged him again and whispered her thanks.

He wrapped his arm around her shoulders and walked with her and Monroe toward the Jeep. "Are you going to explain all this to me?"

"In the car."

Monroe collapsed into the back and Hannah took the front seat beside Liam. Both women wrapped themselves in the blankets Liam produced from his first aid bin. "We need to go straight to see Eddie Conley," Hannah informed him.

Liam, who hadn't even put the key into the ignition, gave Hannah a look of incredulity. "You need a hot shower and dry clothes before anything else."

Hannah shook her head. "You don't understand. I have to explain everything to him before the festival opens."

"You'll have time to do that after you warm up. Because of the rain, Harry White pushed the festival opening to five o'clock. The sun had already broken through in Blackberry Valley when I left, so the fields should have time to dry enough by then."

Hannah exhaled in relief. "Monroe, is that okay with you? We'll take time to clean up and then meet at your grandparents' house?"

"Yes, but when are you going to explain everything to Liam and me?"

"As soon as I send a few texts to set everything up. Promise." She reached in her pocket automatically, and then reality hit. "Oh. No phone."

Liam handed her his phone as he started the car. "Use this, but I hope you know the numbers."

"I don't. Monroe, do you know your grandfather's number?"

"Yes, but he doesn't check messages. Text Nana and tell her to have Grandpa call."

Hannah chafed at the delay, but there wasn't much choice. She also had to contact Junior, but she had no idea how.

Liam drove for about fifteen minutes before pulling off the road to stop for coffee at a convenience store. "No arguments. You need something to warm you."

While Liam and Monroe went inside, Hannah toyed with Liam's phone. There was one person she had been able to rely on all her life.

Dad picked up on the first ring. "Liam, is Hannah okay?"

"Hi, Dad. Sorry to scare you. I had a mishap with my phone, so I'm using Liam's. I need a huge favor."

Hannah could feel the weight of relief in his words. "Anything for my girl. As long as you promise you're okay."

"I am. I need you to locate Junior Burton and relay a message for me. This sounds cryptic, but it's really important. Tell him it's time to get his dad and be at Eddie's by two o'clock. Please give him Liam's number and tell him to call me on it if he has any questions."

"*I* have a ton of questions, but I doubt you'll answer them at the moment."

"By tonight, you'll know everything." These secrets had been kept long enough.

Dad agreed. As soon as they hung up, Liam's phone rang with a number just one digit off from the one she had used to message Beverly.

"Liam Berthold's phone. This is Hannah speaking."

Eddie's voice came through loud and puzzled. "Hannah? Beverly told me to call this number for you, but she didn't tell me why."

"She didn't know why." Hannah sucked in a breath. "Eddie, I have your answers. I don't want to tell you over the phone because there are really three parts and three different people involved. You need to hear it in their words, or as close to them as possible."

There was a long silence, but eventually Hannah heard the words that lightened her heart. "If I've waited fifty years, I guess I can wait a little longer. How is this going to work?"

"I need to meet with you before the festival starts tonight. It's pushed back until five because of the weather. I'm going to be at your house shortly before two so I can explain everything."

Hannah disconnected the call, then leaned back in the seat and closed her eyes. She'd wanted to tell him and Beverly to expect visitors, but knowing Beverly, she'd feel obligated to put on a feast. Better to let it be just one more surprise, for which Hannah would hopefully be forgiven.

Chapter Twenty-Eight

Hannah jolted awake as Liam's Jeep pulled up behind the Hot Spot. She rubbed her eyes and, hearing the crinkle of the silver blanket, blinked in confusion.

"You fell asleep before I even got back with your coffee. Monroe went out soon after." He indicated her friend, still asleep in the back seat. "If I didn't know it was a stress reaction, I'd have thought you were trying to avoid telling us what's going on."

Hannah started to smile, but it turned into a yawn. "Last thing I remember is talking to Eddie. He's expecting me before two. What time is it now?"

"Just after noon."

"Oh, wow. I have to hurry."

"Hannah." Liam laid a hand on her arm. "Relax. You're alive. Praise the Lord for that. The rest will work out according to His plan."

Liam's words gave her pause. "You're absolutely right." She took a deep breath and let it out slowly. "Do you have to go back to work, or can you come with me to Eddie's?"

"I'll drop Monroe off and come back for you."

Hannah started to protest that it was too much trouble, but he stopped her. "I want to do it, Hannah. Humor me."

In that moment, Hannah realized just how scared her fiancé had been. It was sobering. "Okay. I'll go take that shower and have coffee." She picked up the cold paper cup. "Maybe I'll make a fresh cup."

Liam laughed. "I'll be back for you in plenty of time. No need to rush. And take this. It's a cheap phone from the convenience store to tide you over until you can replace yours." He handed her a small bag.

She leaned across the console to kiss him. "You definitely are my favorite fiancé, even if this phone doesn't say so."

Liam grinned. "Oh, it does."

Hannah was still laughing as she opened the back door and climbed the stairs to her apartment. The first thing she planned to do was check in with Junior. She could get his number from the cloud backup information on her laptop. Then a shower, then coffee.

Then it would be showtime.

Hannah and Liam climbed the steps to Eddie and Beverly's front porch with a few minutes to spare. Junior had promised to have his father there at exactly two. Hannah hoped she had enough time to prepare Eddie so he didn't turn them away.

Beverly was fluttery with nerves when she opened the door, so Hannah took a moment to calm her. "It will be all right. But you can say a prayer for your husband to be forgiving."

Beverly swallowed hard as she nodded. Then she escorted Hannah and Liam to the study where Eddie waited with Monroe and Sandy, tapping his foot and plucking at the upholstery on his chair in the way Hannah imagined he'd once picked his mandolin.

"Hi, Eddie. You know my fiancé, Liam Berthold, don't you?"

"I do. He's a lucky man."

Liam shook Eddie's hand. "Yes, I am, sir. Good to see you again. My grandfather sends his regards."

"Well, you give him mine right back. It would be nice to see Patrick again."

"I'll make that happen. Now, Hannah has some important news, even if she wouldn't tell me what it is."

Liam's comment drew laughter from everyone, which was just what they'd needed to ease the tension. Hannah pulled up a hassock and sat down in front of Eddie. She closed her eyes long enough to utter a prayer that she would be given the right words to make peace for all these hurting people.

Then she began. "I know the answers to the mystery of what happened that final day of the festival fifty years ago. It turns out, there were actually three different mysteries that needed to be solved."

Beverly gasped, but Hannah saw Monroe grasp her nana's hand to comfort her. Eddie's eyes widened, but he didn't say a word.

"I'll start with the mandolin, which was an unfortunate accident." Her temporary phone dinged, and she glanced down. Right on time. "I could tell you what happened, but I think it will be better for everyone concerned if you hear it from the man who has been haunted by the secret for fifty years."

Eddie harumphed, but didn't object.

"I asked that person to meet me here. With your permission, I'll bring him in. Eddie, I believe it would be better for you to speak in private."

Beverly murmured a protest, but Eddie nodded. "You've worked a miracle. I'll trust whatever you ask."

At that pronouncement, the others left the room. Hannah leaned over to him. "Then I ask only that you listen with an open heart."

From the expression in his watery eyes, Hannah wondered if he had an inkling of who he was about to see.

She got up and headed out front to welcome Junior and his father. The elderly man looked none too happy to be there, and Junior looked like he might be sick at any moment. Hannah gave him a hug to boost his morale. "He's ready to see you."

Without further ado, she ushered them down the hall and into the study. "Eddie, Junior Burton is here to explain to both you and his father what happened."

Once the two Burton men had entered the room, Hannah closed the door behind them. She leaned back against the heavy wood and offered a fervent prayer for peace and understanding.

Hannah was sorely tempted to listen at the keyhole, but she had just put it in God's hands. Her job was to explain to the others in attendance. Earlier, she had asked Liam to keep them away from the front hall and study, so she found them in the kitchen where Beverly was arranging food with the help of her daughter, Sandy. Monroe paced. Only Liam looked calm. He trusted her.

Hannah walked to the table and suggested that they join her. Once they were seated, she began. "Right now Junior Burton and his father are in the study. Junior can finally confess to Eddie that he accidentally broke his mandolin fifty years ago during the dinner break and was too scared to admit it." She waited until the murmurs subsided. "I'm hoping that Eddie will understand that he was just a frightened boy and forgive Junior so that he and Ward can finally make peace. But even if he can't, at least he'll finally know."

"Did Junior steal the money too?" Sandy asked.

"No," Monroe answered. "Hannah figured that part out too."

"If we can wait to see how things go in the study, I'd prefer to explain to everyone at once."

They sat together for almost twenty minutes, everyone watching the minutes tick by on the big kitchen clock.

At long last, Junior appeared in the doorway. The relief on his face told Hannah everything she needed to know.

Beverly must have seen it too, because she rushed to him and enveloped him in a hug. "You poor boy."

He squeezed his eyes tight and hugged her back. "Dad and Eddie are waiting for you to tell the rest of the story, Hannah."

They all headed back down the hall, but Hannah hung back with Beverly. "You knew?"

Beverly gave Hannah a gentle smile. "I wondered. Maybe even suspected, but I didn't know." Hannah mentally filled in the missing words. Beverly had been too busy keeping her own secret to risk digging into someone else's.

When Hannah walked into the study with Beverly, she was delighted to see Liam chatting with Ward and Eddie. The room fell silent as they noticed her. When Eddie beamed at her, tears rushed to Hannah's eyes. She blinked them back. "And now for the rest of the story. We should all sit down for this part."

When everyone was once again settled, Hannah told the story, beginning with what Shelby had confessed to her and ending with that morning's meeting with Maureen and Hilary. "After I leave here, I'll meet with Sheriff Steele to give him the evidence. He and the prosecutor will have to decide what to do. I don't know if Shelby

Lowe has the right to any input, but I would like yours. I promised Maureen's daughter that I would relay her story as well, so I will."

She went on to explain how desperately Maureen had wanted to escape her family legacy and make a new life for herself. "Hilary claims that, except for this aberration, her mother led an exemplary life. That, of course, doesn't change the fact that Maureen committed a felony, so it'll be up to the prosecutor, then a judge or jury, to decide whether she'll serve time."

Eddie glanced at Ward. "Can't speak for my partner here, but I'm in a rather forgiving mood at the moment. You can tell the sheriff he has my support to go easy on her if he feels it is the right thing."

Ward was quiet for long enough that Hannah began to get nervous. Finally, he said, "I've had enough bad blood with the Hughes family that I truly understand her need to escape. I don't condone her methods, but I'm with Eddie. The money being stolen wasn't what hurt us. It was losing our friendship. And that was all on us." He leaned over and rested a hand on Eddie's shoulder. "I think in the past fifty years, we've all learned a lot about what really matters in life. If the sheriff thinks Maureen has too, you'll get no objection from me."

His words were met with a round of cheers, but Ward wasn't finished. "Hannah, I haven't had the pleasure of knowing you except for our brief video call, but from what my son has told me, the credit for our reunion goes to you. So, from the bottom of this grateful man's heart, I say thank you. I wish I had a way to repay you."

"I know of a way," Monroe said, with a twinkle in her eye. "But I'm going to make her wait the way she made me."

There was another round of laughter, then Eddie raised his hand to speak. He bowed his head, drew a breath, and began. "For fifty years, I've been considered the victim in this tragedy. I've struggled mightily with that because I was not without fault, as was proven today. Junior has lived with guilt for fifty years because my anger prevented him from confessing. Ward bore the burden of my accusations." Eddie turned to his former partner. "I'm truly sorry, my friend. I lashed out at you when I was hurt, rather than leaning on our friendship to get through it. I overreacted to losing the mandolin, but that was because I could. What I couldn't rage about publicly was my pain and guilt for hurting the person who was most dear to me." He had eyes only for Beverly as he spoke. "You've carried your secret for years, but I always knew."

Beverly covered her face with trembling hands.

Eddie stood, crossed the room, and put his arms around her. "I am sorry I made you feel unloved, that I put my music before you. It took almost losing you to open my eyes, but the night the mandolin disappeared, I only knew the fear. That was what I was really so upset about. It took me weeks to figure out how to rebuild what we almost lost." He turned back to Junior. "You might have broken my mandolin, Junior, but you saved my marriage. Thank you. I am so grateful for what you did."

Chapter Twenty-Nine

Later Saturday night Hannah disconnected her phone call and hurried back to rejoin Liam in the festival crowd.

He greeted her with an expectant look. "From your expression, I'm guessing the call went well?"

She burst into an even bigger smile. "As well as anyone could hope. Colin spoke with the prosecutor. Of course they still have to interview everyone involved, but so far they think it can be resolved with restitution and house arrest. Maureen will literally pay the price, but she won't spend time behind bars. I'm glad about that."

"Me too." Liam wrapped his arm around her. "And now we can enjoy the rest of the festival."

Monroe was just finishing up a set with her band, and her mother came out on the stage to join her for the next act.

Hannah tapped her toes and hummed along until the music came to an end.

Monroe took the microphone from its stand and stepped forward. "Good evening. I hope you're all having fun. Are you?"

A roar of approval went up from the crowd.

When the noise finally died down, Monroe went on. "It's been fifty years since the last bluegrass festival in Blackberry Valley, and I speak for all of us performing tonight when I say we are so glad Harrison White decided to revive the tradition."

There was another round of applause before Monroe continued. "It's been a great night, wouldn't you agree?"

Hannah laughed and leaned up to murmur in Liam's ear as the audience cheered again. "She's eating this up."

"Well, it's about to get even better!" Monroe announced. "Ladies and gentlemen, thanks to the amazing detective skills of our very own Hannah Prentiss, I am thrilled to announce that for the first time in five decades, Blackberry Valley is going to hear the music of none other than the original Blackberry Mountain Boys. Give it up for Ward Burton and Eddie Conley!"

Hannah gasped. "I didn't know they agreed to perform."

Liam hugged her and laughed. "Monroe said you'd have to wait for your thank-you."

Hannah's eyes were full of happy tears as Eddie and Ward took the stage to momentous applause.

Monroe had one last thing to say. "Hannah, this song is for you."

The first notes of "Blue Moon of Kentucky" filled the air, and Hannah could barely contain herself. Ward and Eddie played their hearts out. As she watched, Hannah could see them as they must have been fifty years ago, full of youthful energy. The sounds they drew from their instruments were mesmerizing.

Hannah leaned her head against Liam's shoulder, and he held her close. "I'm so proud of you," he said. "They owe this all to you."

Hannah let out a contented sigh. "It's all God's perfect timing."

There had been times over the past week when she'd feared the worst from her investigation. But instead of breaking hearts and dividing families, the truth had opened doors, rebuilt bridges, and resulted in the beautiful music they were so blessed to enjoy this evening.

She offered a prayer of thanksgiving as Ward and Eddie were joined onstage by all the performers. The opening notes of the "Swing Low, Sweet Chariot" medley filled the air, and the crowd sang along.

Liam rested his cheek against her hair and murmured, "I hope this is the first of many annual festivals, so that someday we can bring our children out to experience true bluegrass."

Hannah beamed up at him. "From your lips to God's ears."

From the Author

Dear Reader,

I have such happy memories of coming home from work on Friday evenings and knowing that my husband was already there, because I could hear the voices of Dolly Parton or Emmylou Harris greeting me from upstairs. After a hard week's work, that Boston boy loved to kick back and relax with bluegrass or country music.

When I was developing this story, my oldest daughter dug out those old CDs to help inspire me. It worked! Listening to all the bluegrass greats from Bill Monroe, Flatt and Scruggs, the Osborne Brothers, Alison Krauss, Dolly, Emmylou, and so many more helped me fall into the story. I hope you could feel my love for the music as you read, and that maybe it inspired you to go have a listen yourself.

It's been such fun visiting with Hannah, Liam, Lacy, and the gang again. I hope you enjoy reading the Mysteries of Blackberry Valley as much as I've enjoyed writing them.

Signed,
Cate Nolan

About the Author

Once upon a time, there was a girl who loved to read more than anything, and she especially loved mysteries. That girl, Cate Nolan, grew up to write her own stories. Today she is a *Publishers' Weekly* bestselling author of suspense and mystery novels.

Although Cate spent most of her life in New York, she now lives by the sea in Maine, where the rolling waves and foggy mornings inspire her. When she's not writing, Cate is a Middle School English Language Arts teacher who encourages her students to develop their own reading and writing talents.

The Hot Spotlight

The Story of Bluegrass

One of my favorite things about writing is when research supplies the answer to plot questions. When I was researching bluegrass music and history in preparation for writing this story, I discovered the rift that was caused by advancing technology. Depending on your take, traditional bluegrass either resisted advances in technology or utilized those same advances to expand the audience at a time when artists were competing with the rise of rock and roll.

For those unfamiliar with bluegrass, let's take a quick look at this unique music's history.

Bill Monroe is often regarded as the father of bluegrass, because he was the person who created and cultivated what he called the "pure music" of bluegrass from the traditions of hillbilly, folk, and gospel music.

Groups like Monroe's Blue Grass Boys in the 1940s traditionally included band members playing acoustic guitar, banjo, mandolin, upright bass, and fiddle. These instruments, combined with vocals, helped create that "high lonesome sound" bluegrass is known for.

Bluegrass enjoyed popularity in the fifties and sixties, with festivals hitting their heyday in the sixties and seventies. But then along came rock and roll.

Rock music didn't challenge the style of bluegrass, which remained well-loved, but the electrified sound brought controversy. Should bluegrass bands remain true to their tradition and sound even if it limited the audience, or should they jump on the amplification bandwagon to attract larger crowds in major arenas?

There was no right answer, and bands chose their own paths, but some groups did split up when members couldn't agree. However, change has always been a constant in bluegrass groups. Bands form and disband, members join and move on. But through all the transitions, one thing remains true—bluegrass music gives us a unique and catchy sound that will have you tapping your feet and wanting to listen again and again.

From the Hot Spot Kitchen

SWEET CAROLINE'S BLACKBERRY JAM CAKE

Jam Cake

Ingredients:

1 cup (2 sticks) unsalted butter

2 cups granulated sugar

3 large eggs, beaten

1¼ cups buttermilk

1 teaspoon baking soda

1 cup seedless blackberry jam

3½ cups all-purpose flour

1 teaspoon cinnamon

1 teaspoon ground cloves

1 teaspoon ground allspice

1 teaspoon vanilla extract

1 cup chopped black walnuts or pecans

Directions:

1. Preheat oven to 350 degrees. Grease and flour two 9-inch cake pans or a tube pan.
2. With an electric mixer, beat butter and sugar until light and creamy. Add eggs.
3. Beat in buttermilk, baking soda, and jam until well blended.

4. Whisk together flour and spices in a separate bowl. Slowly add to batter, beating until combined.
5. Add nuts and mix.
6. Divide batter evenly between the 9-inch pans or pour it all into the tube pan.
7. Bake 30 to 40 minutes (9-inch pans) or 40 to 50 minutes (tube pan).
8. Test for doneness with a toothpick inserted in center of cake.
9. Cool 10 to 15 minutes in pan and then turn onto rack for further cooling.

Blackberry Cream Cheese Icing

Ingredients:

½ cup (1 stick) butter, softened

8 ounces cream cheese, softened

1 teaspoon vanilla extract

3 teaspoons seedless blackberry jam, plus more for spreading between layers

6 cups powdered sugar

Directions:

1. Cream butter and cream cheese with electric mixer until smooth.
2. Add vanilla and jam, and mix thoroughly.
3. Gradually add powdered sugar to reach desired consistency.
4. For 9-inch cakes, spread a thin layer of icing and another layer of blackberry jam on one cake. Place other cake layer over jam and generously ice entire cake. For bundt cake, drizzle icing and jam over cake as desired. Garnish with fresh blackberries.

Read on for a sneak peek of another exciting book in the *Mysteries of Blackberry Valley* series!

Forged in Fire

BY STEPHANIE COLEMAN

The longer Hannah Prentiss sat at the table with bookkeeper Rusty Studebaker, the lighter her heart felt. Why had she waited so long to get help with managing the Hot Spot finances?

Both her fiancé, Liam Berthold, and her best friend, Lacy Minyard, had been telling her for months that she should outsource this part of owning a restaurant. Lacy had gone so far as to share stories about how much more relaxed her husband, Neil, was since he'd hired Rusty. Finally, Hannah had agreed to meet with him, and now she couldn't believe she'd put this off for so long. While neither Liam nor Lacy were likely to say, "I told you so," Hannah wouldn't blame either of them if they did.

As Rusty wrapped up his explanation of the best way for Hannah to scan and send him receipts, she released an intentionally dramatic sigh. "Rusty, I think you're an answer to prayer."

He chuckled. "I'll have to tell my mother you said that. She wanted me to go into ministry. I'm not sure she's ever believed that accounting can be the Lord's work too."

Hannah sipped her sweet tea. "I'm certainly glad He gifted you with numbers, because that's not the way He gifted me."

"You're being too hard on yourself." Rusty popped a french fry into his mouth. Hannah was sure that by now it was too cold to be any good, but he didn't complain. "You may not enjoy bookkeeping work, but you've done a fine job keeping up with it. You'd be surprised how many small business owners have called me in a panic, and I find they've never recorded a single thing."

Hannah felt a touch of pride at Rusty's compliment. He reminded her of her father in many ways, though Rusty was probably only in his fifties. But, like Gabriel Prentiss, Rusty was generous with compliments and laughter. And when he smiled, his eyes crinkled in the same way as her dad's.

Raquel Holden materialized at the table, holding a to-go box and wearing her usual warm smile. "Here's that fried chicken salad for you, sir. Anything else I can get for either of you?"

Hannah smiled at her. Raquel's black curls were pulled back into a jaunty ponytail that suited her well, and she wore a touch of shimmery eye makeup that made her dark eyes seem even livelier than usual. "Nothing for me. Thanks, Raquel."

"Me neither," Rusty said.

Raquel headed for a table of newly seated guests perusing their menus.

Rusty tapped the to-go box. "My wife will be thrilled. Thank you so much. You're sure I can't pay for it?"

Hannah shook her head, sending her blond hair swaying. "Not a chance. This meeting has taken a huge weight off my shoulders."

"I'll be a hero when I walk in the door holding this. Pamela told me she had a dream about this salad last night. That's how much she loves it."

"It's our most popular salad this summer. I think it's the candied bacon."

"We don't make it into Blackberry Valley as often as we'd like." Rusty slid his laptop into his bag and stood. "Our house is in the country, but Cave City is a bit closer, so that's where we typically end up when we need groceries or a quick bite to eat. They don't have anything like the Hot Spot there, though."

"Did Pamela grow up in Blackberry Valley as well?"

"Nope, just me." Rusty slung the strap of his bag over his shoulder and gazed out the tall, wide front windows of the Hot Spot. "I enjoy living there, but I do miss being in town sometimes. Still feels like home when I'm here."

Hannah followed his gaze out to Main Street. Today was the seventh of July, and the Americana banners and decorations from the annual Fourth of July celebration still lined the street. Despite the heat and humidity, July was a picturesque month in Blackberry Valley, with flowers in bloom and the trees a vibrant green.

Hannah and Rusty exchanged warm farewells, and then he was gone, taking with him one of the most dreaded recurring tasks on her to-do list. She couldn't stop smiling.

"Good meeting?" asked Elaine Wilby, the Hot Spot hostess.

"Fantastic. I think he's going to be a huge help."

Elaine grinned and tucked her dark hair behind her ears. "I like hearing that. Now that you're running the Hot Spot plus planning a wedding, I've been a little worried about your stress level."

"Me too," Hannah admitted.

She had imagined planning a wedding would feel romantic and exciting—and it did sometimes, but it also felt overwhelming. Even though neither she nor Liam wanted an elaborate celebration, it was hard to plan something "simple" when they both had deep roots in the community. And Hannah had quickly learned that any size and scale of wedding involved an abundance of choices.

Hannah leaned against the hostess stand. "Though this week I'll be spending more time getting ready for Lacy's baby shower than I will doing things for the wedding."

Elaine clapped her hands together, her dark brown eyes shining. "I still can't believe how close the Minyards are to having their baby."

Hannah grinned so hard her cheeks hurt. She'd never been so excited to throw a party. Every time she thought about snuggling her best friend's newborn baby, a thrill ran through her. Hannah loved babies, and she loved Lacy and Neil, so this was as exciting as the anticipated arrivals of her niece and nephews years before.

"I'm so excited that I maybe got too ambitious planning the food for Sunday," she said with a chuckle. "It's hard for me to restrain myself when it comes to themed food."

"What's the theme?"

"The farm." Lacy owned and operated Bluegrass Hollow Farm, which supplied fresh eggs to the Hot Spot as well as to plenty of other customers.

"That's perfect," Elaine said. "Do you want some extra help?"

Hannah waved away the offer. "You don't need to do that."

"I know, but I want to. What if I take care of the decorating so you can focus on the food?"

Hannah hesitated. She'd always been much better at offering help to others than she was at accepting it.

"Please?" Elaine persisted. "I love decorating, and you have enough to do getting the food ready. Let me help."

The shower was happening a few hours after church in her apartment above the Hot Spot, and a set of extra hands would be nice.

"If you're sure you don't mind..." Hannah hedged.

"Are you kidding? Decorating for a baby shower is a delight. What time do you want me here?"

"Maybe twelve thirty? The shower starts at two."

Elaine pulled her phone from her pocket. "I'm putting it in my calendar now. Do I need to pick up decorations, or did you already buy some?"

"Everything has been purchased. I'm not sure how long the actual decorating will take, but I'm sure there will be plenty to do. Thank you so much, Elaine."

"Thanks for letting me help."

Elaine put her phone away as the doors opened. A young couple came inside, holding hands and gazing dreamily at each other.

Elaine smiled at them as she gathered menus. "Welcome to the Hot Spot. Table for two?"

Hannah's phone buzzed in her back pocket, but she waited until Elaine had led the couple away before she pulled it out to check who was calling. She'd anticipated the call being from Liam, who'd left that morning along with his best friend and fellow firefighter, Archer Lestrade, to help with raging wildfires in Wyoming. Hannah was so proud of them for voluntarily heading up there to help, but saying goodbye that morning had felt harder than she'd anticipated.

She blinked a few times at the screen, which didn't say *Liam "My Favorite Fiancé" Berthold*, but instead read *Aunt Fiona*. Aunt Fiona was her mother's younger sister, and while she sent occasional emails and texts, Hannah couldn't remember the last time she'd received a phone call from her. Was something wrong?

Hannah swiped to answer the call. "Hello?" she said in a slightly breathless voice as she stepped outside into the soupy afternoon heat.

"Hannah!" Aunt Fiona's high-pitched voice sounded chipper, not distressed. "I wasn't sure if you'd be able to answer your phone during business hours."

"You caught me at a good time, fortunately. Though I did assume something was wrong when I saw you were calling."

Aunt Fiona laughed. "Isn't that sad? We all think the worst when we get phone calls these days. How is my favorite restaurateur doing? Is that the right term?"

"You nailed it. I'm good." Hannah considered the potted geraniums Elaine had arranged outside the Hot Spot, and pinched off a dead flower. "Maybe a little busier than I'd like to be, but I've never been great at sitting still. How are you?"

"Even as a girl, you were always very busy. I remember one visit when you served me constant cups of pretend tea. Cherry tea, cinnamon tea, grape tea, on and on." Aunt Fiona's voice took on a wistful tone. "Frieda and I laughed and laughed about it. Those were good days."

Hannah wished she could remember serving pretend tea to her mom and her aunt, but her memories didn't stretch back that far. However, she remembered well the joy she always felt as a child when she heard Aunt Fiona was coming for a visit. Her mother's sister didn't come often, but she always arrived ready to have fun.

"That's actually related to why I'm calling," Aunt Fiona continued. Her voice had the same husky tone that Hannah's did whenever she was fighting off tears. "I turn fifty-six next week, and it has me thinking about Frieda almost constantly. I'll be turning the same age as my big sister, and it's strange to think that before long I'll be older than she was. That makes this birthday feel very significant, and I'd like to spend it at home in Blackberry Valley."

"We would love to have you." Hannah's insides fizzed with the anticipation of seeing her mother's only sister again. "You can stay with me."

"You're sure it wouldn't be too much trouble?"

"Of course not. When would you arrive?"

"Is Friday too soon? If I leave DC after breakfast, I could be in Blackberry Valley by dinnertime."

"Friday would be perfect." Hannah couldn't stop grinning. "Aunt Fiona, I'm so excited."

"I am too. I haven't seen you or Gabriel or any of my high school friends in far too long."

Hannah always felt it had been too long since she'd seen Aunt Fiona. Her aunt was one of the coolest people she knew. As a nurse, she'd lived all over the United States. She always had the best stories, the prettiest clothes, and the heartiest laugh. How strange that she had always felt so much younger than Hannah's mother, but was about to turn the same age Mom had been when she'd succumbed to cancer. Hannah had always thought that fifty-six was far too young to die, and the older she got, the truer that seemed.

After saying goodbye, Hannah headed back into the Hot Spot. Just that morning, she'd been thinking how quiet July might feel after Lacy's baby shower. With the Fourth of July festivities over, Liam out of town being his wonderful heroic self, and the next menu change for the Hot Spot still weeks away, Hannah had foreseen lots of time alone at her apartment, working on wedding plans.

But with Aunt Fiona coming to town, there was no chance that life in Blackberry Valley would feel "quiet" at all.

Loved *Mysteries of Blackberry Valley?*
Check out some other Guideposts mystery series!

Whistle Stop Café Mysteries

Join best friends Debbie Albright and Janet Shaw as they step out in faith to open the Whistle Stop Café inside the historic train depot in Dennison, Ohio. During WWII, the depot's canteen workers offered doughnuts, sandwiches, and a heap of gratitude to thousands of soldiers on their way to war via troop-transport trains. Our sleuths soon find themselves on track to solve baffling mysteries—both past and present. Come along for the ride for stories of honor, duty to God and country, and of course fun, family, and friends!

Under the Apple Tree
As Time Goes By
We'll Meet Again
Till Then
I'll Be Seeing You
Fools Rush In
Let It Snow
Accentuate the Positive
For Sentimental Reasons

That's My Baby

A String of Pearls

Somewhere Over the Rainbow

Down Forget-Me-Not Lane

Set the World on Fire

When You Wish Upon a Star

Rumors Are Flying

Here We Go Again

Stairway to the Stars

Winter Weather

Wait Till the Sun Shines

Now You're in My Arms

Sooner or Later

Apple Blossom Time

My Dreams Are Getting Better

Secrets from Grandma's Attic

Life is recorded not only in decades or years, but in events and memories that form the fabric of our being. Follow Tracy Doyle, Amy Allen, and Robin Davisson, the granddaughters of the recently deceased centenarian, Pearl Allen, as they explore the treasures found in the attic of Grandma Pearl's Victorian home, nestled near the banks of the Mississippi in Canton, Missouri. Not only do Pearl's descendants uncover a long-buried mystery at every attic exploration, they also discover their grandmother's legacy of deep, abiding faith, which has shaped and guided their family through the years. These uncovered Secrets from Grandma's Attic reveal stories of faith, redemption, and second chances that capture your heart long after you turn the last page.

History Lost and Found
The Art of Deception
Testament to a Patriot
Buttoned Up
Pearl of Great Price
Hidden Riches
Movers and Shakers
The Eye of the Cat
Refined by Fire

The Prince and the Popper

Something Shady

Duel Threat

A Royal Tea

The Heart of a Hero

Fractured Beauty

A Shadowy Past

In Its Time

Nothing Gold Can Stay

The Cameo Clue

Veiled Intentions

Turn Back the Dial

A Marathon of Kindness

A Thief in the Night

Coming Home

Savannah Secrets

Welcome to Savannah, Georgia, a picture-perfect Southern city known for its manicured parks, moss-covered oaks, and antebellum architecture. Walk down one of the cobblestone streets, and you'll come upon Magnolia Investigations. It is here where two friends have joined forces to unravel some of Savannah's deepest secrets. Tag along as clues are exposed, red herrings discarded, and thrilling surprises revealed. Find inspiration in the special bond between Meredith Bellefontaine and Julia Foley. Cheer the friends on as they listen to their hearts and rely on their faith to solve each new case that comes their way.

The Hidden Gate
A Fallen Petal
Double Trouble
Whispering Bells
Where Time Stood Still
The Weight of Years
Willful Transgressions
Season's Meetings
Southern Fried Secrets
The Greatest of These
Patterns of Deception

MYSTERIES OF BLACKBERRY VALLEY

The Waving Girl
Beneath a Dragon Moon
Garden Variety Crimes
Meant for Good
A Bone to Pick
Honeybees & Legacies
True Grits
Sapphire Secret
Jingle Bell Heist
Buried Secrets
A Puzzle of Pearls
Facing the Facts
Resurrecting Trouble
Forever and a Day

Mysteries of Martha's Vineyard

Priscilla Latham Grant has inherited a lighthouse! So with not much more than a strong will and a sore heart, the recent widow says goodbye to her lifelong Kansas home and heads to the quaint and historic island of Martha's Vineyard, Massachusetts. There, she comes face-to-face with adventures, which include her trusty canine friend, Jake, three delightful cousins she didn't know she had, and Gerald O'Bannon, a handsome Coast Guard captain—plus head-scratching mysteries that crop up with surprising regularity.

A Light in the Darkness
Like a Fish Out of Water
Adrift
Maiden of the Mist
Making Waves
Don't Rock the Boat
A Port in the Storm
Thicker Than Water
Swept Away
Bridge Over Troubled Waters
Smoke on the Water
Shifting Sands
Shark Bait

Seascape in Shadows
Storm Tide
Water Flows Uphill
Catch of the Day
Beyond the Sea
Wider Than an Ocean
Sheeps Passing in the Night
Sail Away Home
Waves of Doubt
Lifeline
Flotsam & Jetsam
Just Over the Horizon

A Note from the Editors

We hope you enjoyed another exciting volume in the Mysteries of Blackberry Valley series, published by Guideposts. For over seventy-five years, Guideposts, a nonprofit organization, has been driven by a vision of a world filled with hope. We aspire to be the voice of a trusted friend, a friend who makes you feel more hopeful and connected.

By making a purchase from Guideposts, you join our community in touching millions of lives, inspiring them to believe that all things are possible through faith, hope, and prayer. Your continued support allows us to provide uplifting resources to those in need. Whether through our communities, websites, apps, or publications, we inspire our audiences, bring them together, and comfort, uplift, entertain, and guide them. Visit us at guideposts.org to learn more.

We would love to hear from you. Write us at Guideposts, P.O. Box 5815, Harlan, Iowa 51593 or call us at (800) 932-2145. Did you love *The Mandolin Mystery*? Leave a review for this product on guideposts.org/shop. Your feedback helps others in our community find relevant products.